LifeChange

A NAVPRESS BIBLE STUDY SERIES

A life-changing
encounter with God's Word

ECCLESIASTES

Money. Sex. Power. Experiences. Knowledge.
What happens when we reach
the end of those things?

A NavPress resource published in alliance
with Tyndale House Publishers, Inc.

NavPress is the publishing ministry of The Navigators, an international Christian organization and leader in personal spiritual development. NavPress is committed to helping people grow spiritually and enjoy lives of meaning and hope through personal and group resources that are biblically rooted, culturally relevant, and highly practical.

For more information, visit www.NavPress.com.

For information about special discounts for bulk purchases, please contact Tyndale House Publishers at csresponse@tyndale.com, or call 1-800-323-9400.

ISBN 978-1-61521-735-9

Printed in the United States of America

24	23	22	21	20	19	18
9	8	7	6	5	4	3

CONTENTS

HOW TO USE THIS GUIDE

Although the LIFECHANGE guides vary with the individual books they explore, they share some common goals:

1. To provide you with a firm foundation of understanding, plus a thirst to return to the book throughout your life

2. To give you study patterns and skills that help you explore every part of the Bible

3. To offer you historical background, word definitions, and explanation notes to aid your study

4. To help you grasp the message of the book as a whole

5. To teach you how to let God's Word transform you into Christ's image

As You Begin

This guide includes eight lessons that will take you chapter by chapter through all of Ecclesiastes. (Ecclesiastes has twelve chapters, so an alternative structure and approach for this study is to devote a weekly lesson to each of those chapters, making a full twelve-week study. For the lessons in this book that currently cover two chapters in Ecclesiastes, you'll find clear breaks where the focus shifts from one chapter to the next.) To benefit most from this time, here's a good way to begin your work on each lesson:

1. Pray for God's help to keep you mentally alert and spiritually sensitive.

2. Read attentively through the entire passage mentioned in the lesson's title.

(You may want to read the passage from two or more Bible versions—perhaps at least once from a more literal translation such as the New International Version, English Standard Version, New American Standard Bible, or New King James Version, and perhaps once more in a paraphrase such as *The Message* or the New Living Translation.) Do your reading in an environment that's as free as possible from distractions. Allow your mind and heart to meditate on the words you encounter—words that are God's personal gift to you and all His people.

After reading the passage, you're ready to dive into the numbered questions for the chapter, which make up the main portion of each lesson. Each of the questions is followed by blank space for writing your answers. This act of writing your answers helps clarify your thinking and stimulates your mental engagement with the passage as well as your later recall. Use extra paper or a notebook if the space for recording your answers seems too cramped. Continue through the questions in numbered order. If any question seems too difficult or unclear, just skip it and go on to the next.

Most of the questions will direct you back to Ecclesiastes to look again at a certain portion of the assigned passage for that lesson. At that point, be sure to use a more literal Bible translation rather than a paraphrase.

As you look closer at the passage, it's helpful to approach it in this progression:

Observe. What does the passage actually *say*? Ask God to help you see it clearly. Notice everything that's there.

Interpret. What does the passage *mean*? Ask God to help you understand. And remember that any passage's meaning is fundamentally determined by its *context*. Stay alert to all you see about the setting and background of Ecclesiastes, and keep thinking of the book as a whole while you proceed through it chapter by chapter. You'll be progressively building up your insights and familiarity with what it's all about.

Apply. Keep asking yourself, *How does this truth affect my life?* Pray for God's help as you examine yourself in light of that truth and in light of His purpose for each passage.

Try to consciously follow all three of these approaches as you shape your written answer to each question in the lesson.

The Extras

In addition to the regular numbered questions you see in this guide, each lesson also offers several questions or suggestions that appear in the margins. All of these will appear under one of three headings:

Optional Application. Try as many of these questions as you can without overcommitting yourself, considering them with prayerful sensitivity to the Lord's guidance.

For Thought and Discussion. Many of these questions address various ethical issues and other biblical principles that lead to a wide range of implications. They tend to be particularly suited for group discussions.

For Further Study. These often include cross-references to other parts of the Bible that shed light on a topic in the lesson, plus questions that delve deeper into the passage.

(For additional help in effectively studying the Bible, refer to the "Study Aids" section beginning on page 123.)

Changing Your Life

Don't let your study become an exercise in knowledge alone. Treat the passage as God's Word, and stay in dialogue with Him as you study. Pray, "Lord, what do You want me to notice here?" "Father, why is this true?" "Lord, how does my life measure up to this?" Let biblical truth sink into your inner convictions so you'll increasingly be able to act on this truth as a natural way of living.

At times you may want to consider memorizing a certain verse or passage you come across in your study, one that particularly challenges or encourages you. To help with that, write down the words on a card to keep with you, and set aside a few minutes each day to think about the passage. Recite it to yourself repeatedly, always thinking about its meaning. Return to it as often as you can for a brief review. You'll soon find the words coming to mind spontaneously, and they'll begin to affect your motives and actions.

For Group Study

Exploring Scripture together in a group is especially valuable for the encouragement, support, and accountability it provides as you seek to apply God's Word to your life. Together you can listen jointly for God's guidance, pray for each other, help one another resist temptation, and share the spiritual principles you're learning to put into practice. Together you affirm that growing in faith, hope, and love is important and that you need each other in the process.

A group of four to ten people allows for the closest understanding of each other and the richest discussions in Bible study, but you can adapt this guide for other-sized groups. It will suit a wide range of group types, such as home Bible studies, growth groups, youth groups, and church classes. Both new and mature Christians will benefit from the guide, regardless of their previous experience in Bible study.

Aim for a positive atmosphere of acceptance, honesty, and openness. In your first meeting, explore candidly everyone's expectations and goals for your time together.

A typical schedule for group study is to take one lesson per week, but feel free to split lessons if you want to discuss them more thoroughly. Or omit some questions in a lesson if your preparation or discussion time is limited. (You can always return to this guide later for further study on your own.)

When you come together, you probably won't have time to discuss all the questions in the lesson, so it's helpful to choose ahead of time the ones you want to make sure to cover thoroughly. This is one of the main responsibilities that a group leader typically assumes.

Each lesson in this guide ends with a section called "For the Group." It gives advice for that particular lesson on how to focus the discussion, how to apply the lesson to daily life, and so on. Reading each lesson's "For the Group" section ahead of time can help the leader be more effective in guiding the group.

You'll get the greatest benefit from your time together if each group member also prepares ahead of time by writing out his or her answers to each question in the lesson. The private reflection and prayer that this preparation can stimulate will be especially important in helping everyone discern how God wants you to apply each lesson to your daily lives.

There are many ways to structure the group meeting, and in fact you may want to vary your routine occasionally to help keep things fresh.

Here are some of the elements you can consider including as you come together for each lesson:

Pray together. It's good to pause for prayer as you begin your time together. When you begin with prayer, it's worthwhile and honoring to God to ask especially for His Holy Spirit's guidance of your time together. If you write down each other's prayer requests, you are more likely to remember to pray for them during the week, ask about them at the next meeting, and notice answered prayers. You might want to get a notebook for prayer requests and discussion notes.

Worship. Some groups like to sing together and worship God with prayers of praise.

Review. You may want to take time to discuss what difference the previous week's lesson has made in your life as well as recall the major emphasis you discovered in the passage for that week.

Read the passage aloud. Once you're ready to focus attention together on the assigned Scripture passage in the week's lesson, read it aloud. (One person could do this, or the reading could be shared.)

Open up for lingering questions. Allow time for the group members to mention anything in the passage that they may have particular questions about.

Summarize the passage. Have one or two people offer a summary of the passage.

Discuss. This will be the heart of your time together and will likely take the biggest portion of your time. Focus on the questions you see as the most important and most helpful. Allow and encourage everyone to be part of the discussion for each question. You may want to take written notes as the discussion proceeds. Ask follow-up questions to sharpen your attention and deepen your understanding of what you discuss. You may want to give special attention to the questions in the margin under the heading "For Thought and Discussion."

Encourage further personal study. You can find more opportunities for exploring the lesson's themes and issues under the marginal heading "For Further Study" throughout the lesson. You can also pursue some of these together, during your group time.

Focus on application. Look especially at the "Optional Application" sections found in the margins. Keep encouraging one another in the continual work of adjusting your lives to the truths God gives in Scripture.

Summarize your discoveries. You may want to read the passage aloud one last time together, using the opportunity to solidify your understanding and appreciation of it and clarify how the Lord is speaking to you through it.

Look ahead. Glance together at the headings and questions in the next lesson to see what's coming next.

Give thanks to God. It's good to end your session by pausing to express gratitude to God for His Word and for the work of His Spirit in your minds and hearts.

Keep these worthy guidelines in mind throughout your time together:

Let us consider how we may spur one another on toward love and good deeds.

(HEBREWS 10:24)

Carry each other's burdens, and in this way you will fulfill the law of Christ.

(GALATIANS 6:2)

Accept one another, then, just as Christ accepted you, in order to bring praise to God.

(ROMANS 15:7)

THE BOOK OF ECCLESIASTES

The Quest for Meaning

Many Bible readers would agree that Ecclesiastes "is one of the most puzzling books of the Bible."[1] "It is best to be frank from the outset: Ecclesiastes is a difficult book."[2] Because of its challenges and uniqueness, studying Ecclesiastes is particularly interesting as well as challenging. Yet perhaps this book isn't really so hard to understand as we're sometimes conditioned to believe. "Despite the attempts of biblical scholars and others to make the book seem problematical and inaccessible, it is an easy book to read and grasp."[3] "Once we see what is broadly happening in the book, it is not too difficult to find our way about it."[4]

For Reflection Today

"The book of Ecclesiastes has been aptly called the most contemporary or modern book in the Bible."[5]

"Ecclesiastes was clearly written as a discussion guide for people prepared to think out their response to God's unseen hand in life and history."[6] It is the "thinking man's book."[7] "The book is God's wise counsel for those who know His ways but have found them perplexing and troubling."[8]

"The theme of Ecclesiastes is the necessity of fearing God in a fallen and therefore frequently confusing and frustrating world."[9]

The Quest

What we find in Ecclesiastes "is a virtual summary of the biblical worldview: life lived by purely human and earthly standards is empty, while life with God at the center is fulfilling."[10]

The author of Ecclesiastes "in effect tells the story of his quest to find satisfaction in life. This quest is reconstructed from the vantage point of someone whose quest ended satisfactorily. The transitions between units often keep the quest in view: 'so I turned to consider,' 'again I saw,' 'then I saw,' etc. As the quest unfolds, one is continuously aware of the discrepancy between the narrator's present outlook and his futile search undertaken in the past. In effect, the speaker recalls the labyrinth of dead ends that he pursued, recreating his restless past with full vividness but not representing it as his mature outlook."[11]

"Ecclesiastes grapples with the question of how people should live in a world where the good Creator and just Judge sovereignly ordains that "bad" things happen to the righteous as well as to the wicked, and not according to what they deserve. The gift of contentment is to be exercised not only in the face of human oppression but under the futility and death that God imposed upon the human race because of sin."[12]

The author of Ecclesiastes "is demolishing to build. The searching questions he has asked are those that life itself puts to us, if we will only listen. He can afford to ask them, because in the final chapters he has good news for us, once we can stop pretending that what is mortal is enough for us, who have been given a capacity for the eternal."[13]

"We face the appalling inference that nothing has meaning, nothing matters under the sun. It is then that we can hear, as the good news which it is, that *everything* matters—'for God will bring every deed into judgment, with every secret thing, whether good or evil.' That is how the book will end. On this rock we can be destroyed: but it is rock, not quicksand. There is the chance to build."[14]

"In summary, Ecclesiastes teaches how God's elect, pilgrims in this world 'under the sun' (1 Peter 1:1), but also citizens of heaven (Philippians 3:20), should live amid the profound frustrations and tensions of the present evil age (Romans 8:18-23)."[15]

Understandably, our thoughts turn to Christ as we wrestle honestly with the difficulties of life presented in Ecclesiastes. "The book of Ecclesiastes has been called a Christ-shaped vacuum. Its contribution to the story line of the Bible is to record the longing of the human soul to find satisfaction and to point us toward the satisfaction of that longing in a Christ-centered experience of life. Jesus is the meaning of life, and if he is not at the center of our daily experience, we will find only futility and frustration."[16]

Author

The opening line of the book tells us that these are the words of the "son of David, king in Jerusalem." This phrasing immediately brings to mind David's son Solomon, but Ecclesiastes—unlike Proverbs and the Song of Songs—never actually mentions the name *Solomon*. "Strictly speaking . . . the book is anonymous, given that no personal name is attached to it. Nevertheless, traditional Jewish and Christian scholarship has often ascribed authorship to Solomon."[17] "To many interpreters of Ecclesiastes, the lineage (1:1), kingship in Jerusalem (1:1,12), unsurpassed wisdom (1:16), and rivaled wealth (2:4-9) of the author indicate that Solomon, calling himself 'the Preacher' [or 'Teacher'] (1:12), is the author of Ecclesiastes."[18]

Solomon's authorship of the book has often been questioned, although "there are, in fact, no passages in the book that rule out the possibility of Solomonic authorship."[19] But no other possibilities have gained wide acceptance among Bible scholars.

"It is best simply to recognize that some interpreters have concluded the author was Solomon, while others think it was some other writer later than Solomon. Regardless, the book claims that its wisdom ultimately comes from the 'one Shepherd' (12:11), i.e., from God."[20]

"The fact of the matter" is that the author "is all but completely veiled behind the text of Ecclesiastes. . . . All the emphasis falls on the words, not the speaker."[21]

Structure: Moods and Cycles

One way to catch a big-picture perspective of Ecclesiastes is to identify alternating passages where the "dominant mood" is either positive or negative. We thus recognize the book as "a prolonged contrast between two viewpoints. In terms of space, the major theme is the emptiness of life under the sun — that is, life lived by merely human and earthly values. The counterpart, which is intertwined and does not (contrary to a common misconception) surface only at the end, asserts an alternative to life at ground level. We might call it life above the sun: a God-centered view that opens the door to finding meaning in the earthly sphere.

"The book shuttles back and forth between negative and positive sections. The key to interpreting the parts of the book accurately is to note into which of the two contexts a passage falls. The writer himself gives us hints in this regard. The phrase 'under the sun' or an equivalent appears conspicuously in the negative sections. The positive sections, which are briefer than the negative ones (like a breath of fresh air), refer conspicuously to God. The negative passages tell us the truth just as thoroughly as the positive sections do: they tell us the truth about life without God."[22]

This approach is represented in the following chart:[23]

Passage	Subject Matter	Dominant Mood
1:1-3	Introduction to author and theme	Negative
1:4–2:23	Life under the sun: meaningless cycles; pursuit of knowledge, pleasure, wealth, work	Negative
2:24-26	Life above the sun: the God-centered life	Positive
3:1-22	Two views of time	Positive
4:1–5:17	Life under the sun: how life fails to satisfy	Negative
5:18-20	Life above the sun: the God-centered life	Positive

Passage	Subject Matter	Dominant Mood
6:1–9:6	Life under the sun: the disappointments and disillusionments of life	Negative
9:7-10	The enjoyment of life	Positive
9:11–10:20	Life under the sun: disillusionment and folly	Negative
11:1–12:8	How to live well despite the limitations that are inevitable parts of life	Positive
12:9-14	Wrap-up: concluding thoughts	Positive

"Assertions made in the 'under the sun' passages do not represent the author's final viewpoint, whereas those that appear in the positive passages do."[24]

Another view of the book's structure recognizes three major "cycles" in the content, set within a frame:[25]

I.   Introduction (1:1)
II. Motto (1:2)
III. First Cycle: Limitations of work and wisdom (1:3–3:8)
IV. Second Cycle: Work in fear before God, whose work endures (3:9–6:7)
V.   Third Cycle: Wisdom in humility before a judging God, whose wisdom is unfathomable (6:8–12:7)
VI. Motto (12:8)
VII. Conclusion (12:9-14)

Still another approach[26] sees a two-part "discourse" set within the frame:

I.   Author (1:1)
II. Theme: The meaninglessness of man's efforts on earth apart from God (1:2)
III. Introduction: The profitlessness of working to accumulate things to achieve happiness (1:3-11)
IV. Discourse, Part 1: In spite of life's apparent enigmas and meaninglessness, it is to be enjoyed as a gift from God (1:12–11:6)
V.   Discourse, Part 2: Because old age and death will soon come, man should enjoy life in his youth, remembering that God will judge (11:7–12:7)
VI. Theme Repeated (12:8)
VII. Conclusion: Reverently trust in and obey God (12:9-14)

These various outlines show that while "no consensus has been reached about the book's structure,"[27] organizing patterns are nevertheless there in the text to help us perceive the message of Ecclesiastes.

1. J. Stafford Wright, *Ecclesiastes*, Expositor's Bible Commentary, vol. 5, ed. Frank E. Gabelein (Grand Rapids, MI: Zondervan, 1991), 1137.
2. Iain Provan, *Ecclesiastes/Song of Songs*, The NIV Application Commentary (Grand Rapids, MI: Zondervan, 2001), 23.
3. Leland Ryken and Philip Graham Ryken, eds., *The Literary Study Bible* (Wheaton, IL: Crossway, 2007), introduction to Ecclesiastes, "The Book at a Glance."
4. Derek Kidner, *The Message of Ecclesiastes*, The Bible Speaks Today, ed. J. A. Motyer (Downers Grove, IL: InterVarsity, 1976), 14.
5. Ryken and Ryken, introduction to Ecclesiastes, "The Book at a Glance."
6. Wright, 1138.
7. Darryl DelHousaye, *Today for Eternity* (Sisters, OR: Questar, 1991), January 19.
8. *New Geneva Study Bible* (Nashville: Thomas Nelson, 1995), introduction to Ecclesiastes, "Date and Occasion."
9. *ESV Study Bible* (Wheaton, IL: Crossway, 2008), introduction to Ecclesiastes, "Theme and Interpretation of Ecclesiastes."
10. Ryken and Ryken, introduction to Ecclesiastes, "The Book at a Glance."
11. *ESV Study Bible*, introduction to Ecclesiastes, "Literary Features."
12. *New Geneva Study Bible*, introduction to Ecclesiastes, "Characteristics and Themes."
13. Kidner, 19.
14. Kidner, 20.
15. *New Geneva Study Bible*, introduction to Ecclesiastes, "Characteristics and Themes."
16. Ryken and Ryken, introduction to Ecclesiastes, "Ecclesiastes as a Chapter in the Master Story of the Bible."
17. *ESV Study Bible*, introduction to Ecclesiastes, "Author, Title, and Date."
18. *New Geneva Study Bible* (Nashville: Thomas Nelson, 1995), introduction to Ecclesiastes: "Author."
19. Wright, 1140.
20. *ESV Study Bible*, introduction to Ecclesiastes, "Author, Title, and Date."
21. Provan, 29.
22. Ryken and Ryken, introduction to Ecclesiastes, "The Book's Dialectical Structure."
23. Ryken and Ryken, introduction to Ecclesiastes, "The Book's Dialectical Structure."
24. Ryken and Ryken, introduction to Ecclesiastes, "Tips for Reading Ecclesiastes."
25. *New Geneva Study Bible*, introduction to Ecclesiastes, "Outline."
26. *NIV Study Bible* (Grand Rapids, MI: Zondervan, 1985), introduction to Ecclesiastes, "Outline."
27. *New Geneva Study Bible*, introduction to Ecclesiastes, "Characteristics and Themes."

ECCLESIASTES 1

The Nearest Thing to Zero

1. For getting the most from Ecclesiastes, one of the best guidelines is found in 2 Timothy 3:16-17, words Paul wrote with the Old Testament first in view. He said that *all* Scripture is of great benefit to (a) teach us, (b) rebuke us, (c) correct us, and (d) train us in righteousness. Paul added that these Scriptures completely equip the person of God "for every good work." In which of these areas do you especially want to experience the usefulness of Ecclesiastes? Express your desire in a written prayer to God.

For Thought and Discussion: What previous impressions have you had of the book of Ecclesiastes?

_____

_____

_____

_____

_____

2. In Jeremiah 23:29, God says that His Word is like fire and like a hammer. He can use the Scriptures to burn away unclean thoughts and desires in our hearts. He can also use Scripture, with hammer-like hardness, to crush and crumble our spiritual hardness. From your study of Ecclesiastes, how do you most want to see the "fire-and-hammer" power of God's Word

Optional Application: We read that after Jesus' resurrection, when He was explaining Old Testament passages to His disciples, He "opened their minds so they could understand the Scriptures" (Luke 24:45). Ask God to do that kind of work in *your* mind as you study Ecclesiastes so you're released and free to learn everything here He wants you to learn and so you can become as bold, worshipful, and faithful as those early disciples of Jesus. Express this desire to Him in prayer.

at work in your own life? Again, express this longing in a written prayer to God.

_____

_____

_____

_____

_____

_____

3. Think about these words of Paul to his younger helper Timothy: "Do your best to present yourself to God as one approved, a worker who does not need to be ashamed and who correctly handles the word of truth" (2 Timothy 2:15). As you study God's Word of truth in Ecclesiastes, he calls you to be a "worker." It takes *work*—concentration and perseverance—to fully appropriate God's blessings for us in this book. Express here your commitment before God to work diligently in this study of Ecclesiastes.

_____

_____

_____

_____

_____

4. If you're already somewhat or partially familiar with the book of Ecclesiastes, which passages in it are your favorites?

_____

_____

_____

_____

_____

5. Glance ahead through the pages of Ecclesiastes. What are some of the recurring phrases, thoughts, and ideas that you observe again and again?

_____

_____

_____

_____

6. From what you see in 2:26, 3:12, 5:19, 7:14, and 11:9, how would you summarize the kind of teaching that the book of Ecclesiastes appears to give about happiness or joy?

_____

_____

_____

_____

7. Find the most prominent activity that reccurs in the following verses: 2:24; 3:13; 4:9; 5:19; 8:15; 10:15. What clues could this offer about the central message of Ecclesiastes?

_____

_____

_____

_____

8. Look at the word that is repeated in 1:2. Then scan the rest of the book to notice how frequently it is used in Ecclesiastes. What do you know about the meaning of this word as it is used here in Ecclesiastes?

_____

_____

_____

_____

9. What do you discover in 11:9 and 12:1 about the intended audience for this book?

_____

_____

_____

_____

10. What evidence do 1:1, 1:12-13, 1:16, 2:1-9, and 12:9-10 provide in helping us identify the author of this book?

_____

_____

_____

_____

Teacher ["Preacher," ESV, NKJV] (1:1). "There is a certain mystery about this writer's way of announcing himself; and this intriguing touch is not likely to be unintentional."[1] The Hebrew term here is transliterated as "Qohelet" (or "Qoheleth," "Kohelet," "Koheleth"). This word "is generally taken to denote the function of one who addresses a *qahal*, 'assembly.'"[2] In the Septuagint, the ancient Greek translation of the Old Testament, this was translated as *Ekklesiastes*, a Greek word meaning "speaker of a called-out assembly."[3]

"The Preacher is not to be viewed as some kind of skeptical iconoclast but rather as a teacher of orthodoxy, whose musings on God and human existence present a consistent message that is to be viewed as standing within the broad stream of the biblical wisdom tradition. . . .

"At the same time, however, the Preacher is distinctly original and creative in his thought and manner of expression and is not merely restating what other sages have taught. As a genuine wisdom teacher, he has a gift for penetrating observation and for stating things in a profound and challenging manner that spur the listener on to deeper thought and reflection."[4]

Son of David (1:1). See also Matthew 1:1.

"The Teacher, writing as a wise and observant king of David's line [1:1, 12-13], set out his theme."[5]

11. What seem to be the various possible shades of meaning to the phrase "Everything is meaningless" in 1:2?

_____

_____

_____

_____

Meaningless! Meaningless! ["Vanity of vanities," ESV, NKJV] (1:2; see also 12:8). The Hebrew term used here is "notoriously difficult to translate. Literally the word means 'vapor' and conjures up a picture of something fleeting, ephemeral, and elusive, with different nuances to be ascertained from each context."[6] "One's understanding of this important thematic statement will significantly influence one's interpretation of the book as a whole."[7] The Hebrew term "commonly has the figurative use of that which is

Optional Application: As you reflect on the opening words of Ecclesiastes, especially in verse 2 of chapter 1, use their message to prompt your continued prayer. "Life is like a vapor or breath, passing too quickly for you and me to figure out — but not for the eternal God who created it. Don't try to understand it all yourself. Ask God to teach you about it, to open your mind to things you might be afraid to think about."[8]

For Further Study:
Reflect on the fact that the Hebrew term translated in Ecclesiastes as "meaningless" (NIV) or "vanity" (ESV, NKJV) has the primary meaning of "vapor" or "breath." How do you see this concept also in Job 7:16, Psalm 39:5, and James 4:14?

For Further Study:
How might Romans 8:20 relate to what is being expressed in Ecclesiastes 1:2?

evanescent and unstable. . . . The thought of futility may be read into most occurrences of the word in Ecclesiastes."[9] "A wisp of vapor, a puff of wind, a mere breath—nothing you could get your hands on; the nearest thing to zero. That is the 'vanity' this book is about. What makes this reading of life disturbing is that this airy nothingness is not seen as a mere flicker on the surface of things, where it might even have had a certain charm. It is the sum total."[10]

"Solomon is saying, 'Vapor of vapors, the thinnest of all vapor—so is life.' It passes so quickly that to try figuring it out is futility; it will appear senseless to one who sees it go by like a breath of air.

"Solomon's intent in Ecclesiastes is *not* to say life is hopeless, but to help us understand how life 'under the sun' is to be lived if you truly want to enjoy it. This book tells us that life is given by God as a gift and that He has a plan for it all. But Solomon focuses first on the fact that the distracting restlessness within and around us keeps us from enjoying life.

"Ask yourself, How can I focus my motion so that everything has a reason—and the reason is Jesus?"[11]

12. What legitimate answers come to mind for the question the author of Ecclesiastes asks in 1:3?

_____

_____

_____

_____

Gain [NIV, ESV; "profit," NKJV] (1:3). "The Hebrew
word here . . . is a commercial term referring to
'the value left over.'"[12] The term is used eigh-
teen times in Ecclesiastes (including 2:11,13;
3:9; 5:9,16; 7:11; 10:10). The author uses it "in
the manner of 'advantage,' 'gain,' or 'profit.' . . .
Proverbs points out there is advantage in toil
over laziness (Proverbs 14:23). But Ecclesiastes
probes deeper by continually asking what profit
does one gain from his toil (Eccles. 1:3; Eccles.
3:9). The answer is nothing, especially if it is
to accumulate goods which cannot be taken at
death (Eccles. 2:11; Eccles. 5:15). Ecclesiastes
here feels the full force of the curse on man's
work which makes it toil and he clearly sees
that ultimate value cannot reside in man's
labor or its results."[13]

For Further Study:
How would you com-
pare Ecclesiastes 1:3
with Paul's explana-
tion of labor and toil
in Colossians 1:28-29?

What do we "gain" (Ecclesiastes 1:3)? "After it's
all over, what's in life for me? Will I receive a just
return for my investment? Or is life cheating
me? What's left after all that energy goes into
life? What do we achieve for all our sweat and
stress?"[14]

Under the sun (1:3). In Scripture this phrase is
found only in Ecclesiastes, where it occurs
twenty-nine times. Its use "shows that the
writer's interest was universal and not limited
to only his own people and land."[15] "This
phrase is synonymous with 'under heaven' and
'on earth.' Paul's equivalent is 'this present evil
age' (Galatians 1:4). The energies poured into
earthly kingdoms are often of no value to the
kingdom of heaven (Mark 8:36). By contrast,
the work of the Lord is not in vain (John 6:27-
29; 1 Corinthians 15:58)."[16] "The phrase *under
the sun* does not indicate a 'secular' point
of view, as is often claimed (the Preacher's
frequent references to God exclude such an
interpretation) but rather refers to the world
and to mankind in their current fallen state."[17]
"It makes clear enough that the scene in mind

For Further Study:
Compare the message of Ecclesiastes 1:4-8 with what you see in Psalm 19. What further reason do we see for the cyclical motion in nature and in our lives?

is exclusively the world we can observe, and that our observation point is at ground level."[18]

13. As a possible statement of the theme of the entire book, how would you express the meaning of 1:1-3 in your own words?

_____

_____

_____

_____

14. Apart from the context of the surrounding verses, the message of verses 4-7 in Ecclesiastes 1 might seem to be positive, not negative. How would you express what that message is?

_____

_____

_____

_____

15. Think again of the core question in 1:3, *What does man gain?* How would you describe the benefit to humanity of the repetitive processes observed in 1:4-7?

_____

_____

_____

_____

"Solomon was interested in nature generally (see 1 Kings 4:33). The scientist defines physical laws that have always operated; but if we ask him about origins or some ultimate end or purpose, there is nothing he can tell us from nature that will give the meaning of life. The biblical view of nature, however, is that it testifies to a Creator, though it does not compel belief in him (e.g., Psalm 19; Romans 1:20). But the Teacher is concerned with proof rather than testimony and rightly maintains that meaning and security cannot be found in nature alone. If everything is endlessly cyclical, how can man break out of the temporal circle into a state that leads somewhere?"[19]

Optional Application: Reflect deeply on verses 4-8 of Ecclesiastes 1, recognizing the sense in which nature (and all life) can seem so transient, repetitive, aimless, even futile. How have you sensed this in your own life? How do you respond to it emotionally?

16. Even today, what kind of typical experiences and behaviors among humanity would lead an observer to the conclusions seen in Ecclesiastes 1:8?

_____

_____

_____

_____

17. To what extent have you observed the words of 1:9 as being true in life as you have known it? How would you express this observation in your own words?

_____

_____

_____

_____

18. Within your own perspective on truth and human existence, what is your best answer to the question posed in the first half of 1:10?

_____

_____

For Thought and Discussion: What evidence have you seen around you (or in yourself) that human beings are always on the lookout for "something new" (1:10)?

For Further Study: How would you compare the observation and questions in Ecclesiastes 1:10 with what you see in Isaiah 42:9; 43:19; 2 Corinthians 5:17; Revelation 21:5?

Nothing new under the sun (1:9). "How strictly is it meant? Probably our own popular use of it gives the best answer. We exclaim it as a sweeping comment on the human scene, not as a pronouncement about inventions. No one—least of all Qoheleth—is going to deny the inventiveness of man. But . . . the more things change, the more they turn out to be the same. In their new guise the old ways go on. As a race, we never learn."[20]

"'Nothing new. . . . That's what makes life boring, which makes us restless, distracting us from enjoying the gift of life God has given us.

"*But,* you may say, *there are new things to make life exciting — new technologies that open up a whole new future.* No, answers Solomon: 'Already it has existed for ages which were before us' (1:10). New technology in reality only speeds things up — meeting the same old needs and desires faster and perhaps more efficiently, but the needs and desires are still the same: to communicate, to heal, to influence, to destroy. Transcontinental communication is still an extension of the mouth; magnetic resonance imaging is an extension of the eyes; computers are an extension of the mind; intercontinental ballistic missiles are an extension of the fist."[21]

No one remembers the former generations (1:11). In ESV and NKJV, "no remembrance of former things."

Optional Application: To what extent have you also done what the author said he did in the first half of 1:13, or something similar to it? What were the results?

19. Reflect on the statements made in 1:11. In your own observation, how well does humanity remember the people and events of the past? To what degree do you see this as a shortcoming or weakness of humanity?

_____

_____

_____

_____

_____

_____

I . . . was king ["have been king," ESV] (1:12). This may indicate that the time of writing is "at the end of Solomon's life when he cited the fruit of his experiences."[22]

Labors (1:3); ***wisdom*** (1:13). "Ecclesiastes searches for an answer to the question, What is the advantage of humanity's work and wisdom? *Work* and *wisdom* comprise two main themes of the book."[23]

20. From the first half of 1:13, how would you express in your own words what the author did?

_____

_____

_____

_____

21. Think carefully about the statement in the last half of 1:13. What seems to be the nature of this

For Thought and Discussion: With the example of 1:13 in mind, how healthy do you think it is for human beings to actively explore and search out the meaning of human existence? What is the value of this? What, if any, are the drawbacks? Is it possible to be *too* curious about these things?

observation? Would you describe it as more of an emotional perspective, an assertion of fact, a hypothetical assessment, or something else?

_____

_____

_____

_____

_____

I applied my mind ["I applied my heart," ESV; "I set my heart," NKJV] (1:13). "The Hebrew term [for heart] denotes the center of one's inner life, including mind, will, and emotions."[24]

22. The term "meaningless" ("vanity," ESV, NKJV) occurs in 1:14 with the parallel phrase "chasing after the wind" ("striving after wind," ESV; "grasping for the wind," NKJV). How does this second phrase about the wind help us better understand how the author understands the term "meaningless" ("vanity")?

_____

_____

_____

_____

23. In 1:15, what things might the author be referring to as "what is crooked" and "what is lacking"? How does this further amplify the author's use of the term "meaningless" ("vanity")?

_____

_____

_____

_____

I said to myself (1:16). "I said in my heart" (ESV); "I communed with my heart" (NKJV).

Wisdom (1:16). "Qoheleth is taking wisdom with proper seriousness, as a discipline concerned with ultimate questions, not simply a tool for getting things done. . . . But wisdom is concerned with truth, and truth compels us to admit that success can go bad on us, and that nothing on earth has any permanence."[25]

For Further Study: How would you compare the perspective on wisdom and knowledge in 1:16-18 with the Christian perspective in Colossians 2:2-3?

24. What does 1:16 reveal about the author, and why is this information important?

_____

_____

_____

_____

_____

25. How does the author's statement in 1:17 add to or further amplify his statements about himself in 1:13 and 1:16?

_____

_____

_____

_____

I applied myself ["I applied my heart," ESV; "I set my heart," NKJV] (1:17). See also 1:13,16. Note the emphasis on the author's heart in this final section of chapter 1.

26. What is your own response to the author's statement in 1:18?

_____

_____

For Thought and Discussion: What phrases, statements, or concepts in chapter 1 seem to be particularly applicable to our culture today?

_____

_____

_____

27. How do you see Christ as the missing link and the fulfillment for the particular vacuum the author of Ecclesiastes has observed in chapter 1?

_____

_____

_____

_____

28. What evidence do you see in Ecclesiastes 1 that the author has been on a quest for eternal meaning in life?

_____

_____

_____

_____

29. What would you select as the key verse or passage in Ecclesiastes 1 — one that best captures or reflects the dynamics of what this chapter is all about?

_____

_____

_____

_____

30. List any lingering questions you have about Ecclesiastes 1.

_____

_____

_____

_____

For the Group

In your first meeting, it may be helpful to turn to the front of this book and review together the section "How to Use This Guide."

You may want to focus your discussion for lesson 1 especially on the following issues, themes, and concepts. Which of these are introduced in Ecclesiastes 1?

- The tragic reality of mankind's sinfulness
- The reality of our coming physical death
- Enjoying our work and enjoying life's true pleasures as God's good gifts
- Recognizing life's frustrations and hardships
- The meaning of true wisdom
- Fearing God
- Gratefulness to God

The following numbered questions in lesson 1 may stimulate your best and most helpful discussion: 4, 10, 13, 16, 27, 28, 29, and 30.

Look also at the questions in the margins under the heading "For Thought and Discussion."

1. Derek Kidner, *The Message of Ecclesiastes*, The Bible Speaks Today, ed. J. A. Motyer (Downers Grove, IL: InterVarsity, 1976), 21.
2. J. Stafford Wright, *Ecclesiastes*, Expositor's Bible Commentary, vol. 5, ed. Frank E. Gabelein (Grand Rapids, MI: Zondervan, 1991), 1152.
3. Warren Baker, ed., *The Complete Word Study Old Testament* (Chattanooga, TN: AMG, 1994), introduction to Ecclesiastes.
4. *ESV Study Bible* (Wheaton, IL: Crossway, 2008), introduction to Ecclesiastes, "Theme and Interpretation."
5. Wright, 1152.
6. *ESV Study Bible*, introduction to Ecclesiastes, "Key Themes."
7. *ESV Study Bible*, introduction to Ecclesiastes, "Theme and Interpretation."
8. Darryl DelHousaye, *Today for Eternity* (Sisters, OR: Questar, 1991), January 19.
9. Wright, 1152.
10. Kidner, 22.
11. DelHousaye, February 9.
12. DelHousaye, February 11.
13. Baker, on Ecclesiastes 1:2.
14. DelHousaye, February 11.

15. Wright, 1152.
16. *New Geneva Study Bible* (Nashville: Thomas Nelson, 1995), on Ecclesiastes 1:3.
17. *ESV Study Bible*, on Ecclesiastes 1:3.
18. Kidner, 23.
19. Wright, 1153.
20. Kidner, 26.
21. DelHousaye, February 12.
22. Wright, 1155.
23. *New Geneva Study Bible*, introduction to Ecclesiastes, "Characteristics and Themes."
24. *ESV Study Bible*, note on Ecclesiastes 1:13.
25. Kidner, 31.

ECCLESIASTES 2:1–3:15

Testing and Observing

1. From the first three verses in Ecclesiastes 2, summarize what the author was seeking to learn and experience. What was the author's overall purpose in this search, according to 2:3?

_____

_____

_____

_____

For Thought and Discussion: How would you define "the good life"?

For Further Study: How does the last sentence in Isaiah 22:13 compare with the author's pursuits in Ecclesiastes 2:3?

Pleasure . . . meaningless (2:1). The author "notes at once the 'paradox of hedonism,' that the more you hunt for pleasure, the less of it you find. In any case, he is looking for something beyond it and through it, for this is more than simple indulgence. It is a deliberate flight from rationality, to get at some secret of life to which reason may be blocking the way."[1]

To find out what is good (2:1). The Hebrew word for "find" (*matsa'*) is common throughout Ecclesiastes. Together, this word and the frequent word *hebel* ("meaningless," "vanity") "suggest the fleetingness of any human being's grasp of the full meaning of events."[2]

The author of Ecclesiastes walks a "double path . . . brought out by the following partial translation of 2:1,3: 'I said in my mind, "Come, let me test you with joy and see what is good." . . . I searched with my mind to lead along my body with wine — I myself shepherding my mind with wisdom — and to grasp folly until I saw what was good. . . .' He treads one path with his body while taking another with his mind, hoping in his intoxicated state to experience the full depths of 'folly' and to arrive at discernment."[3]

2. What were his most significant activities and accomplishments as listed in 2:4-8?

_____

_____

_____

_____

Great projects (2:4). "As if he had over-reacted in turning to the futile pleasures, he now gives himself to the joys of creativity. He bends his energies to a project worthy of his aesthetic gifts, his grasp of skills and sciences, and his ability to command a great establishment."[4]

Reservoirs ["pools," ESV, NKJV] (2:6). "Three pools near Bethlehem are said to have been constructed by [Solomon]. . . . Each of the first two can overflow into the pool below it. It is claimed that altogether these pools hold over forty million gallons."[5]

A harem ["many concubines," ESV] (2:8). "Concubinage was considered a legal relationship and not fornication or adultery by the people. Although it was looked on as a normal convention in Old Testament times, it is nowhere ordered by the Lord."[6]

3. What do we learn in 2:9-10 about the *extent* of the author's search and of his endeavors?

_____

_____

_____

_____

Delight in all my labor . . . the reward for all my toil (2:10). See also 2:22-24; 3:22; 5:18; 9:9-10.

For Further Study:
Ecclesiastes mentions the enjoyment of life's pleasures in 2:10. What further biblical insight on this can we gain from Psalm 128:2; Matthew 6:33; 1 Timothy 4:4; James 1:17?

For Further Study:
How does the teaching in Ecclesiastes 2:10-11 compare with the teaching in 1 John 2:15-17?

"He creates a little world within a world: multiform, harmonious, exquisite: a secular Garden of Eden. . . . He has had the sense, for all this, to avoid the rich man's boredom by strenuous activity, enjoyed and valued for its own sake (2:10); and he has kept an appraising eye on his projects, even while in full pursuit of them. 'My wisdom,' he tells us, 'remained with me' (2:9). He has not lost sight of the quest, the search for meaning, which was the mainspring of it all."[7]

4. What was the author's conclusion in 2:11, as expressed in your own words?

_____

_____

_____

_____

_____

For Further Study:
How would you com-
pare the activities
described in 2:1-9
with what we learn
about Solomon in
chapters 3 and 4 of
1 Kings?

"How are the experiences of this rich man to be summed up? More than any other man, he was able to buy every single thing he imagined could satisfy him. He kept his sense of discernment intact (verses 3,9). A critic might say that this prevented him from making a fair sampling of pleasure because constant analysis of one's feelings hinders com-plete enjoyment. But if Solomon had allowed himself to be swept off his feet by sensual pleasures, he would doubtless have sunk to the despair of a slave of immorality. He wanted to determine to what extent one could find the key to life in a varied use of great wealth.

"In the end, money and the pleasures it can buy do not lift us out of the realm of earthbound frustration. . . . Despite riches we may still be empty shells and our gains only as substantial as the wind (verse 11)."[8]

I surveyed all . . . Then I turned my thoughts to consider . . . I saw (2:11-13). The author's quest continues.

Wisdom (2:12). "He is now in a good position . . . to reflect more fully on wisdom in itself."[10]

---

5. How would you describe the "wisdom" that's in view in 2:12-17? What is good about it? What is deficient about it?

_____

_____

_____

_____

_____

_____

For Further Study:
What contrast to 2:11
do you see in the
life of another Old
Testament character,
as recorded in
Hebrews 11:25?

"Gladness of heart, joy, pleasure — it is not that these things are not good in themselves in Ecclesiastes. Yet Qohelet has discovered that the *pursuit* of them with the hope of gain is just as pointless as the pursuit of wisdom and knowledge for that purpose."[9]

The wise man, like the fool (2:16). "In the last analysis, whatever else wisdom can do for one, it can do nothing about the end of life. In that crisis, the wise man is as naked as the fool — and if his wisdom counts for nothing at that point, it is a pretentious failure."[11]

"It is little use commending to us the ultimate worth of wisdom, if in the end none of us will be around to exercise it, let alone to value it. This of course is why the purely human achievements which we call lasting are nothing of the kind. As men of the world we may revere them in this way, but only for lack of Qoheleth's honesty in seeing that *in the days to come all will have been long forgotten* (2:16). He has no illusions. . . .

"So, for the first time in the book but by no means the last, the fact of death brings the search to a sudden stop. If *one fate comes to all,* and that fate is extinction, it robs every man of his dignity and every project of its point."[12]

6. In your own words, how would you describe what is going on in the author's mind and heart as conveyed by his words in 2:17-21?

_____

_____

_____

_____

7. What do you see as the best answer to the question asked by the author in 2:22?

_____

_____

_____

_____

Nothing better (2:24). "The terms 'good' and 'better' always take their significance from their context. Here the reference is not to moral goodness but to functional behavior; i.e., this is the best way for man to pass along the road of life."[13]

To eat and drink and find satisfaction in their own toil (2:24). "To keep the reader rooted in the real world, the author repeatedly uses the imagery of eating, drinking, toil, sleep, death, and the cycles of nature."[14]

From the hand of God (2:24). See also 3:12-13; 9:1. "Life is a gift from God to be enjoyed, yet the enjoyment of it comes only as we see it as a reward from His hand. . . . Pleasure is our reward for good labor, and even the ability to enjoy it comes from Him."[15]

8. a. What does 2:24-26 affirm or imply about God and His nature?

_____

_____

_____

_____

_____

b. What does 2:24-26 affirm about human character and the human condition?

_____

_____

_____

_____

_____

For Thought and Discussion: The author of Ecclesiastes "experienced much of wisdom and knowledge" (1:16) and acknowledged that to those who please Him, "God gives wisdom, knowledge and happiness" (2:26). How would you define the purpose of *wisdom* and *knowledge*?

9. What do you see as the most important words or phrases in 2:24-26, and why?

_____

_____

_____

_____

_____

"For a moment, the veil is lifted in verse 26, to show us something other than futility. The book will end strongly on this positive note, but meanwhile we are shown enough in such glimpses to assure us that there is an answer, and that the author is no defeatist. He disillusions us to bring us to reality."[16]

"Are God's rewards and punishments as clear as verse 26 suggests? The Wisdom writings speak of life in a stable society where individuals and authorities should be carrying out the will of God. . . . The Wisdom writings also recognize that in the world as it is, righteous individuals may suffer as Job did for a time, and that individual sinners may prosper, as Job also pointed out. The Teacher . . . stated God's general plan, which if not fulfilled through society on earth, must be rectified by God in the future judgment (3:16-22; see Matthew 25:28-30). The final sentence at verse 26 obviously refers to the frustration for the sinner."[17]

10. From the words in 2:26, taken together with what you see later in Ecclesiastes in 3:16-17 and 12:14, what are the most important things the author wants his readers to understand about mankind's future judgment from God?

_____

_____

_____

_____

11. What would you select as the key verse or passage in Ecclesiastes 2 — one that best captures or reflects the dynamics of what this chapter is all about?

_____

_____

_____

_____

12. List any lingering questions you have about Ecclesiastes 2.

_____

_____

_____

_____

Ecclesiastes 3:1-15

13. How would you express the overall message of 3:1-8, as it relates to how we live our lives?

_____

_____

_____

_____

There is a time (3:1). See also 3:11,17; 7:14; 8:5-6.

> The poem in Ecclesiastes 3:1-8 is "considered one of the finest pieces of literature ever written." Its phrases come in "fourteen pairs — intensification of the Hebrew number of completion, seven. It is intended to be a representative list of all aspects of living, as if Solomon cut away a section of life for our review and reflection."[18]

14. What is implied in 3:1-8 about mankind's responsibility?

_____

_____

_____

_____

For Further Study: How would you compare the teaching in Ecclesiastes 3:1-8 with what you see in Colossians 4:5 and Ephesians 2:10?

Optional Application: In your own life, what things on the list are you most likely to try to rush (rather than waiting for the proper time)? And what can help you be more patient in this area of life? (Ask God to show you.)

15. Reflect on the words of 3:1-8. What would be some distinctive characteristics and behaviors in the life of someone who truly understands that everything in our lives has its own proper time and season?

_____

_____

_____

_____

16. Do you believe that *every* hour and moment of our lives belongs to an assigned "time" or "season" for some particular God-ordained purpose? Explain the reasoning behind your answer.

_____

_____

_____

"Man is to take his life day by day from the hand of God (2:24-26; 3:12-13), realizing that God has a fitting time for each thing to be done (3:1). The significance of this section [3:1-8] is that man is responsible to discern the right times for the right actions; and when he does the right action according to God's time, the result is 'beautiful' (verse 11)."[19]

17. How might the truth in the first half of 3:2 relate to the controversies in our society today over the sanctity of life?

_____

_____

_____

Time to kill (3:3). "Significantly, the Hebrew word used here for 'to kill' . . . is *not* the word reserved for murder in the sixth commandment, where premeditation seems to be in view (see Exodus 20:13; Deuteronomy 5:17)."[20]

For Further Study:
How does the truth in the last half of 3:3 compare with New Testament teaching in 1 Corinthians 3:10-15 and Galatians 2:18?

18. How might the truth stated in the last half of 3:5 ("a time to embrace and a time to refrain") relate to appropriate standards for sexual behavior?

For Further Study:
What fuller meaning does Jesus give in John 11:35 to the fact that there is "a time to weep" and "a time to mourn" (Ecclesiastes 3:4)?

19. The question asked by the author of Ecclesiastes in 3:9 is quite similar to the one you answered earlier in 2:22. What further perspectives would you add regarding the best way to answer this question?

For Further Study:
How does the truth in the first half of 3:8 ("a time to love and a time to hate") compare with what we're taught in Romans 12:9 and 1 John 4:20?

20. What is this "burden" ("task," NKJV) mentioned in 3:10?

21. In your own words, how would you explain the teaching in 3:10-11 about what God has done?

Optional Application: Reflect deeply on the fact that God "has made everything beautiful in its time" (Ecclesiastes 3:11). Think about what He has made beautiful in your own experience and observation. What things of God-made beauty do you most want to thank God for?

Beautiful (3:11). "Doing the right thing at the right time yields a beautiful sense of fulfillment."[21]

"There is a purpose, a delight, a pleasure, a good reason behind anything and everything that comes into your life. . . . There are no 'oops' in life. This is life— mourning and dancing, silence and speaking, war and peace—and there are appointed times in your life for all of it. Not all of these may appear beautiful in themselves, but when they are seen as parts of the whole work of God, of God's plan, then we understand . . . everything is 'beautiful in its time' (3:11, KJV)."[22]

22. Why do you think the element of "time" is included in the statement in 3:11?

Eternity (3:11). The Hebrew word here "represents 'everness'"[23] It is "a sense of time and future."[24] "We see only part of God's plan, for in this life we are mortal, finite in our existence. Yet we desire to see more. We have an inborn inquisitiveness to learn how everything in our experience can be integrated to make a beautiful whole."[25]

Fathom (3:11). The Hebrew verb "has the sense of 'figure out, comprehend by study' in this verse and other places in the book (7:14,24,26,27,28,29; 8:17)."[26]

Optional Application: How do the observations in 3:12-13 compare with your own experience of work and of life?

23. What does 3:11 teach us about both human capacity and human limitation?

_____

_____

_____

_____

> Ecclesiastes 3:11 "captures the dazzling, bewildering beauty of a world so changeful that its total pattern is beyond us. But pattern it is. We, unlike the animals, can grasp enough to be sure of that, yet never enough to see the whole."[27]

24. How do you see God's grace expressed in 3:12-13?

_____

_____

_____

_____

25. How does 3:12-13 build upon, amplify, or reinforce the earlier message of 2:24-25?

_____

_____

_____

_____

_____

Optional Application: "I know that everything God does will endure forever" (3:14). In your life, what has God done that will last forever?

26. How would you express in your own words the truths about God that are stated in 3:14-15? What do you see as the significance of these truths?

_____

_____

_____

_____

_____

Fear him ["fear before Him," ESV; "fear before him," NKJV] (3:14). "Life remains an enigma . . . until men learn to fear God."[28]

27. According to 3:14, why is it important to fear God?

_____

_____

_____

_____

_____

God will call the past to account (3:15). Or "God seeks what has been driven away" (ESV).

28. What would you select as the key verse or passage in Ecclesiastes 3:1-15 — one that best captures or reflects the dynamics of what these verses are all about?

_____

_____

_____

_____

_____

29. List any lingering questions you have about
    Ecclesiastes 3:1-15.

    _____

    _____

    _____

    _____

For the Group

You may want to focus your discussion for lesson 2
especially on the following issues, themes, and
concepts. Which of these are evident in this section
of Ecclesiastes (2:1–3:15), and how are they further
developed there?

- The tragic reality of mankind's sinfulness
- The reality of our coming physical death
- Enjoying our work, and enjoying life's true plea-
  sures as God's good gifts
- Recognizing life's frustrations and hardships
- The meaning of true wisdom
- Fearing God
- Gratefulness to God

The following numbered questions in lesson 2
may stimulate your best and most helpful discussion: 1, 2, 4, 6, 8, 10, 11, 12, 13, 14, 15, 16, 21, 24,
26, 27, 28, and 29.
Look also at the questions in the margins
under the heading "For Thought and Discussion."

1. Derek Kidner, *The Message of Ecclesiastes*, The Bible
   Speaks Today, ed. J. A. Motyer (Downers Grove, IL:
   InterVarsity, 1976), 31.
2. *ESV Study Bible* (Wheaton, IL: Crossway, 2008), introduction to Ecclesiastes, "Literary Features."
3. Iain Provan, *Ecclesiastes/Song of Songs*, The NIV
   Application Commentary (Grand Rapids, MI: Zondervan,
   2001), 72.
4. Provan, 32.
5. J. Stafford Wright, *Ecclesiastes*, Expositor's Bible Commentary, vol. 5, ed. Frank E. Gabelein (Grand Rapids, MI:
   Zondervan, 1991), 1156.
6. Wright, 1157.

7. Provan, 32.
8. Wright, 1156.
9. Provan, 71.
10. Provan, 75.
11. Kidner, 17.
12. Kidner, 34.
13. Wright, 1160.
14. *ESV Study Bible*, introduction to Ecclesiastes, "Literary Features."
15. Darryl DelHousaye, *Today for Eternity* (Sisters, OR: Questar, 1991), March 19.
16. Kidner, 36.
17. Wright, 1159.
18. DelHousaye, February 28.
19. Wright, 1160.
20. Wright, 1161.
21. Wright, 1162.
22. DelHousaye, February 28.
23. Wright, 1163.
24. *New English Bible* (Oxford: Oxford University Press, 1970), on Ecclesiastes 3:11.
25. DelHousaye, April 22.
26. *ESV Study Bible*, on Ecclesiastes 3:11.
27. Kidner, 16.
28. DelHousaye, April 22.

Lesson Three

ECCLESIASTES 3:16–4:16

Discovering Evil

Ecclesiastes 3:16-22

And I saw something else (3:16). The quest
continues for the author of Ecclesiastes.

1. How do the words in 3:16-17 compare with the
words of Jesus in Matthew 25:28-30?

_____

_____

_____

_____

2. How does 3:16-17 demonstrate the faith of the
author of Ecclesiastes?

_____

_____

_____

_____

**For Thought and
Discussion:** What are
some examples today
of where wickedness
can be observed in
"the place of justice"
(3:16)?

For Thought and Discussion: How important is it for us to have a candid, realistic expectation of physical death (like the viewpoint evidenced in 3:19-20)?

"Most of us behave as though we had endless time and close our eyes to the fact of death. God wants us to face that fact (verse 18). Even in our Christian service of God, there may be the underlying idea that there is still plenty of time tomorrow and what we fail to do here can be made up in our service in paradise. . . .

"We shall not be brought back again for a second chance to cooperate with God in doing his will on this side of eternity (verse 22). . . . We must make the most of the present in order to please God. We cannot count on the future, since we do not know what it is."[1]

3. What reasons does Solomon give in 3:18-21 for the conclusion he reaches in 3:22?

_____

_____

_____

4. How would you explain the "test" that human beings are subjected to according to 3:18-21?

_____

_____

_____

Breath (3:19); ***spirit*** (3:21). These are the same Hebrew word. "There is no reference here to any personal spirit or soul, but the spirit or breath is the sustaining life that comes from God (Genesis 6:17; Psalm 104:29-30)."[2]

---

5. What is your best answer to the question asked in 3:21?

_____

_____

_____

_____

6. What is your best answer to the question asked at the end of 3:22?

_____

_____

_____

_____

7. From what you've seen so far in this book, how would you summarize how the author of Ecclesiastes views the meaning of life?

_____

_____

_____

_____

Ecclesiastes 4

"Although this chapter [Ecclesiastes 4] may seem to be composed of several isolated themes — oppression, envy, individualism — these are linked by the overarching themes of (a) the power complex common among humans and (b) ways of reacting to it."[3]

***Again I looked and saw . . . And I saw . . . Again I
saw*** (4:1,4,7). His quest continues.

---

8. How accurate is 4:1 in describing a continuing
fact in this world?

_____

_____

_____

_____

9. As a response to the statements in 4:1, how
appropriate (in your opinion) are the thoughts
expressed in 4:2-3?

_____

_____

_____

_____

Evil (4:3). "Evil . . . is as tyrannous as death itself,
and even more tragic. The impermanence
of life is sad enough, but its wrongs can be
unbearable."[4]

---

10. When it comes to people's motivations for
the work they do and the things they seek to
accomplish, what evidence have you observed
that might support the statement made in 4:4?

_____

_____

_____

_____

Envy (4:4). "The fuel that feeds the fires of this
human striving after gain is now for the first

time in Ecclesiastes identified (verses 4-6). . . . It is envy that drives us on the mad rush after 'gain.' . . . The suspicion or realization that others are gaining more from life than we are . . . leads us on to compete with them in the insane rat race, striving to outdo them."[5]

For Thought and Discussion: Is there any value at all in being "alone" in the way talked about in Ecclesiastes 4:11? Why or why not?

11. What particular effectiveness do you see in the imagery given in 4:5?

_____

_____

_____

_____

12. What particular effectiveness do you see in the imagery given in 4:6?

_____

_____

_____

_____

13. List the sharp contrasts you see in 4:7-11.

_____

_____

_____

_____

14. How would you summarize the situation being described in 4:7-8, and why does the author of Ecclesiastes disapprove of it?

_____

_____

_____

_____

Optional Application: In what ways would you say that your most valuable relationships reflect the truths being taught in 4:9-12?

For Further Study: As you reflect on the teaching of 4:9-12, how do you see the underlying principles being manifested or reinforced in Genesis 2:18; Proverbs 18:24; 27:6,9,10,14,17; Luke 10:1-3; John 17:21; 1 Corinthians 12:25; Ephesians 4:16?

15. What do you see as the "good return" ("good reward," ESV, NKJV) mentioned in 4:9?

16. In 4:10, what kind of situations might be included in the imagery of a person who "falls"?

"Of course, there's a down side to relationships, a cost to friendship: the loss of independence, the cost of listening, the cost of adjusting to another's lifestyle and having to consult another's feelings, the cost of keeping faith with another's trust.

"But the foundational truth is that it's better not to be alone. It's better to have a friend. . . .

"In this life, you're going to need a little help from your friends. Do you have them in place?"[6]

17. Describe in your own words the positive principle being taught in 4:9-12.

_____

_____

_____

_____

_____

_____

Optional Application: With the teaching of 4:9-12 in mind, think of one step you can take to strengthen one or more of your most important relationships.

___

**Foolish king** (4:13). "Why is he foolish? He 'no longer knows how to receive instruction.' Sometimes having age and position only fossilizes one's self-will. There's more prestige to protect. By not receiving instruction, you no longer have the protection that comes from the counsel of others who have gone before."[7]

"As we grow older, the danger is to grow less teachable. The mind grows narrow and the waistline broader, instead of the other way around. The reason it's hard to remain teachable is that it becomes harder to say you were wrong. Are you a good student? Do you seek counsel? Do you have good counselors in your life?"[8]

19. How would you summarize how this part of Ecclesiastes (3:16–4:16) has helped us gain the understanding this author wants us to have of the "meaninglessness" or "vanity" of life?

_____

_____

_____

_____

20. What would you select as the key verse or passage in this section of Ecclesiastes (3:16–4:16) — one that best captures or reflects the dynamics of what this section of the book is all about?

_____

_____

_____

_____

21. List any lingering questions you have about this section of Ecclesiastes (3:16–4:16).

_____

_____

_____

_____

For the Group

You may want to focus your discussion for lesson 3 especially on the following issues, themes, and concepts. Which of these are evident in Ecclesiastes 3:16–4:16, and how are they further developed there?

- The tragic reality of mankind's sinfulness
- The reality of our coming physical death
- Enjoying our work, and enjoying life's true pleasures as God's good gifts
- Recognizing life's frustrations and hardships
- The meaning of true wisdom
- Fearing God
- Gratefulness to God

    The following numbered questions in lesson 3 may stimulate your best and most helpful discussion: 7, 15, 17, 19, 20, and 21.

    Remember to look also at the "For Thought and Discussion" questions in the margins.

1. J. Stafford Wright, *Ecclesiastes*, Expositor's Bible Commentary, vol. 5, ed. Frank E. Gabelein (Grand Rapids, MI: Zondervan, 1991), 1164.
2. Wright, 1164.
3. Wright, 1165.
4. Derek Kidner, *The Message of Ecclesiastes*, The Bible Speaks Today, ed. J. A. Motyer (InterVarsity, 1976), 18.
5. Iain Provan, *Ecclesiastes/Song of Songs*, The NIV Application Commentary (Grand Rapids, MI: Zondervan, 2001), 104–105.
6. Darryl DelHousaye, *Today for Eternity* (Sisters, OR: Questar, 1991), October 22.
7. DelHousaye, October 23.
8. DelHousaye, October 23.

Lesson Four

ECCLESIASTES 5–6

A Reward of Joy

Ecclesiastes 5

1. Proverbs 2:1-5 tells about the sincere person who truly longs for wisdom and understanding and who searches the Scriptures for it as if there were treasure buried there. Such a person, this passage says, will come to understand the fear of the Lord and discover the knowledge of God. As you continue exploring Ecclesiastes, what "buried treasure" would you like God to help you find here to show you what God and His wisdom are really like? If you have this desire, express it in your own words of prayer to God.

_____

_____

_____

_____

_____

_____

For Further Study: What further insight on the "sacrifice of fools" (Ecclesiastes 5:1) can you discover from 1 Samuel 15:22 and Isaiah 1:11-20?

To listen (5:1). "The Hebrew word for *listen* has a double force—it means to pay attention, and thus *to obey*. The alternative is to offer up 'the sacrifice of fools,' Solomon says: empty worship; rituals without meaning. . . . Worship begins with our mouths closed and hearts and ears open to listen, with the anticipation of obeying."[1]

For Further Study:
How is the teaching about prayer in 5:2 further amplified by what Jesus tells us in Matthew 6:7-13 and by what we read in Romans 8:26?

For Further Study:
How would you compare Ecclesiastes 5:2 with Proverbs 10:19?

For Further Study:
How are the truths of Ecclesiastes 5:1-7 given further weight in the story Jesus tells in Luke 18:9-14?

2. Express in your own words the main things that we're counseled to do in Ecclesiastes 5:1-7 in regard to our relationship with God.

_____

_____

_____

_____

God is in heaven and you are on earth (5:2). "That doesn't mean God is millions of miles away. It means that God is God and you are not. You are not his peer. Remember what humility is all about."[2]

"We are confronted with God at His most formidable: as one who is not impressed by our chatter or by our ritual gifts and airy promises. The opening paragraphs of chapter 5 drive home these points with vigor."[3]

3. What aspects of God's character and personality are highlighted in 5:1-7?

_____

_____

_____

_____

"Life should be marked by acceptance, not by making demands on God. Indeed the God-fearer must continually draw near to God if he is to be sensitive to his will."[4]

Messenger (5:6). The Hebrew word here is used about two hundred times in the Old Testament; in about half of those instances it refers to a human messenger, and in the other half to a messenger from God. "This is one of the few places where it is impossible to say for certain which meaning is intended. The human messenger would be the person who comes to claim the fulfillment of the vow, probably the priest. An angel here would be either one invisibly present as a witness or the recording angel at the Judgment Day."[5]

"Our approach to God must be a realistic response to what he has shown us to be his will. . . . We should try to put ourselves in a position to discover God's way to use what he has given us in our daily life."[6]

4. According to the observations recorded in 5:8-17, why should we not be surprised to see injustice and oppression toward the poor?

_____

_____

_____

_____

5. How does 5:8-17 amplify what the author of Ecclesiastes stated earlier in 2:9-11?

_____

_____

_____

_____

6. What do you see as the most important principles in 5:8-20 regarding our finances, wealth, and work?

Optional Application: How can we be better listeners in God's presence, as we're urged to do in 5:1-7?

For Thought and Discussion: Why do you think fulfilling our vows is so important to God, as we see in 5:4-6? What does this tell us about God's character and also about His standards for us as His children?

Optional Application: Reflect further on 5:4-6. Have you made any vows or resolutions to God that still require further action on your part? If so, how can you bring fulfillment to those obligations? What do you need to do now?

For Further Study: How would you compare 5:3-7 with Proverbs 10:19; 12:13; 18:7; 21:23; James 1:26; 3:1-12?

For Further Study:
How is the teaching of Ecclesiastes 5:10-17 further clarified in 1 Timothy 6:10 and Matthew 6:19-24?

For Further Study:
How would you compare Ecclesiastes 5:15 with Job 1:21?

For Thought and Discussion: In Ecclesiastes 5:18, we see that our "lot" in life includes "toilsome labor." Why do you think it's necessary — from God's perspective — that our lives include hard work?

7. What do you see as the "harm" or "hurt" mentioned in 5:13?

_____

_____

_____

8. In the full context of 5:13-17, what is the danger of accumulated wealth?

_____

_____

_____

_____

I have seen . . . This is what I have observed (5:13,18). His quest continues.

"This is *not* the Epicurean philosophy of 'eat, drink, and be merry, for tomorrow we die.' Our enjoyment includes our *labor,* even our 'toils under the sun' — hard work. Of all the things you've thought to be grateful for, hard work probably isn't one of them.

"Can hard work be enjoyable? Absolutely, when you know you're creating something good, as when your Father in heaven created, and later looked back and said, 'It is good!' God enjoys what He worked to create. . . .

"God has designed us to work — and to feel good about our work. . . . The rewards are in the blessings of the labor and the fruit of our work."[7]

For Further Study:
Think again about Ecclesiastes 5:18-19. "To not work hard is a canker that brings misery to a life. The biblical term for such a person is 'sluggard.' . . . The sluggard hasn't learned that labor is a gift from God's hand."[9] What more can you learn about this from Proverbs 6:9-11; 19:24; 21:26; 22:13; 26:14?

9. According to 5:18-20, what overall approach to life is better than the harmful approaches mentioned in 5:10-17? How would you describe this better approach in your own words?

_____

_____

_____

_____

_____

_____

"The emphasis [in 3:22; 5:18-19; 9:9] lies on enjoyment or joy as itself the reward that we may expect from life and all our effort expended in living it. There is no surplus, no profit beyond that. Indeed, the 'reward' is itself a gift from God, an inheritance in which we share rather than a prize that we earn (see 9: 6). It is in receiving life as a gift from God and in not striving to manipulate it and exploit it in order to arrive at some kind of 'gain' that mortal beings can find contentment."[8]

Gift of God (5:19). "When we begin to see everything as a gift — and not as a prize we have won or a need we expect to have met — there will be gratefulness. And where there is gratefulness, there will be joy."[10]

For Further Study:
How does the attitude toward possessions as seen in 5:19 compare with the example of Christian believers in Hebrews 11:34?

Optional Application: With Ecclesiastes 5:19 in mind, take time to slow down and reflect on what you're grateful for. In this moment, what gifts from God are especially worthy of your thanksgiving?

For Further Study:
How is the teaching in 5:20 further amplified in Deuteronomy 28:47-48; Psalm 19:8; Matthew 25:21; Romans 5:2-3; 5:8-11; Philippians 4:4-7; 1 Thessalonians 5:16-18; Hebrews 12:2; James 1:2-4; 1 Peter 4:13?

"Life just doesn't get simpler. So you have a decision to make: Either drown in the confusion of the complex, or move on to what has been called 'the profound simple.' And what's that? It's taking another look at life and deciding what's really important, what really matters, what truly satisfies my desire to live. And then to get rid of whatever *isn't* important and *doesn't* matter. . . .

"'Do not be anxious for tomorrow,' Jesus said, 'for tomorrow will care for itself.' In Ecclesiastes, Solomon drives home the preciousness of life today. Make it count, every moment! Don't let tomorrow rob you of life today. Too many of us live in the future or past, instead of the present. Don't spend your whole life missing life. Enjoy the good of creation now, for our lives pass quickly, like a vapor. Life is here; life is now. Go ahead and grieve over the suffering, but seize the moment of life, for it is God's precious gift."[11]

10. What does 5:18-20 indicate about God's good desire for our lives, and how can we more fully experience it?

_____

_____

_____

_____

_____

_____

11. What would you select as the key verse or passage in Ecclesiastes 5 — one that best captures or reflects the dynamics of what this chapter is all about?

_____

_____

_____

_____

12. List any lingering questions you have about Ecclesiastes 5.

_____

_____

_____

_____

Ecclesiastes 6

I have seen (6:1). His quest continues.

_____

13. What is the particular "evil" that the author of Ecclesiastes describes in 6:1-6, and why is it evil?

_____

_____

_____

_____

Optional Application: On a typical day, what percentage of your waking hours are spent being "occupied with gladness of heart" (5:20)? Do you think God wants that percentage to be higher in your experience? If so, how do you think it could be increased?

Optional Application: "What are you deferring until later — and why? What could you be enjoying *now* with your family, your friends, but are putting off for no sufficient reason? What good are you being distracted from carrying out? Why defer it until later? (What makes you think there will even be a later?) Why not do it *now*?"[12] What are your best answers for these questions?

Another evil (6:1). "It is not clear . . . that the NIV's 'another' in 6:1, which does not appear in the Hebrew text, is a correct interpretation. We are not dealing here with another 'grievous evil' (verse 2) but are merely exploring further the reality already presented — an evil or bad situation that multiplies just as quickly as

For Thought and Discussion: With Ecclesiastes 6:2 in mind, what do you see as the keys to being able to truly enjoy wealth, possessions, and honor in a God-pleasing way?

For Further Study: How does the situation in Ecclesiastes 6:1-2 compare with the parable Jesus told in Luke 12:15-21?

riches multiply (see 5:11). It is possible to have all that the heart desires (6:2) and yet to find no joy in it."[13]

14. How does 6:2 build upon, amplify, or reinforce the earlier message of Ecclesiastes 5:19?

_____

_____

_____

_____

> Notice the comparison between the man given wealth by God in 5:19 and another man given the same in 6:2. "It seems that 5:19 describes the person who accepts a standard of living for which he has worked, without continually craving for more (see 5:10; 6:9). The man in 6:2 is more concerned with having everything he wants, and his God-given status in life allows this. But inasmuch as his heart is centered on his accumulated wealth, his tragedy comes when God allows this wealth to be taken over by a stranger."[14]

A stillborn child . . . never saw the sun or knew anything, it has more rest (6:3,5). "The point . . . is not to minimize the tragedy of the stillborn child but to emphasize, through the shocking comparison, the tragedy of the life that is lived without contentment or peace of mind (see Job 3:16-19). Such a life could last two thousand years and still be futile (6:6), if the person never learns to 'see the good' (NIV 'enjoy his prosperity')."[15]

"Chapter 6:1-6 . . . makes the point that the more you feel entitled to, and the more you have already, the harder it will seem if God withdraws it, as He may at any moment, and as He ultimately will. For 'do not all go to the one place?' (verse 6) — that is, to the grave."[16]

15. How would you express in your own words the teaching of 6:7-9?

_____

_____

_____

_____

16. What do you see as the best answers to the two questions asked in 6:8?

_____

_____

_____

_____

17. How is the brevity of our lives emphasized in 6:10-12?

_____

_____

_____

_____

18. How might the teaching in 6:10 confirm that God is sovereign and has predestined all things?

_____

_____

_____

_____

19. How does 6:11 build upon or amplify or reinforce the earlier message of Ecclesiastes 5:1-7?

_____

_____

_____

_____

The more the words, the less the meaning (6:11).
"The more words, the more vanity" (ESV).

"The first question of 6:12 ('Who knows what is good for a man in life?') is not meant to imply a complete lack of human knowledge about what is good, but is intended only to remind us of its contingent and limited nature" — something that is "already clear from everything that has preceded this verse in the book. Throughout his discourse on human folly and misery, and even as he has touched on the folly of expecting too much of wisdom (1:12-18; 2:12-16), Qohelet has never deviated from his conviction that some ways of being are better than others — indeed, wisdom is better than folly — and that the good life is bound up with knowing and accepting that this is so (e.g., 2:13,24-26; 3:12-13,22; 4:6,9,13; 6:9)." This point will be "underlined in the opening verses of chapter 7."[17]

20. What are your best answers to the two questions asked in 6:12?

_____

_____

_____

_____

21. What would you select as the key verse or passage in Ecclesiastes 6 — one that best captures or reflects the dynamics of what this chapter is all about?

_____

_____

_____

_____

22. List any lingering questions you have about Ecclesiastes 6.

_____

_____

_____

_____

For the Group

You may want to focus your discussion for lesson 4 especially on the following issues, themes, and concepts. Which of these are evident in Ecclesiastes 5 and 6, and how are they further developed there?

- The tragic reality of mankind's sinfulness
- The reality of our coming physical death
- Enjoying our work, and enjoying life's true pleasures as God's good gifts
- Recognizing life's frustrations and hardships
- The meaning of true wisdom
- Fearing God
- Gratefulness to God

The following numbered questions in lesson 4 may stimulate your best and most helpful discussion: 2, 3, 6, 8, 9, 10, 11, 12, 17, 20, and 21.

Remember to look also at the "For Thought and Discussion" questions in the margins.

1. Darryl DelHousaye, *Today for Eternity* (Sisters, OR: Questar, 1991), October 28.
2. DelHousaye, October 29.
3. Derek Kidner, *The Message of Ecclesiastes*, The Bible Speaks Today, ed. J. A. Motyer (Downers Grove, IL: Inter-Varsity, 1976), 14.
4. J. Stafford Wright, *Ecclesiastes*, Expositor's Bible Commentary, vol. 5, ed. Frank E. Gabelein (Grand Rapids, MI: Zondervan, 1991), 1167.
5. Wright, 1168–1169.
6. Wright, 1168.
7. DelHousaye, November 24.
8. Iain Provan, *Ecclesiastes/Song of Songs*, The NIV Application Commentary (Grand Rapids, MI: Zondervan, 2001), 74.
9. DelHousaye, November 24.
10. DelHousaye, November 25.
11. DelHousaye, January 20.
12. DelHousaye, January 20.
13. Provan, 129.
14. Wright, 1171.
15. Provan, 130.
16. Kidner, 16.
17. Provan, 139.

ECCLESIASTES 7

Living in the Present

The last verse of chapter 6 raised the question of what is *good* for us in our earthly lives, which pass so quickly. The counsel in chapter 7 appears as a response to that question.

1. In the opening verses of chapter 7, a number of things are said to be "better" than something else. Identify and explain these comparisons in the following passages:

7:1 _____

_____

_____

_____

7:2 _____

_____

_____

_____

7:3-4 _____

_____

_____

_____

For Further Study: How would you compare Ecclesiastes 7:1 with Proverbs 22:1?

Optional Application: Is the wisdom mentioned in 7:4 a wisdom that you are sharing in? In what way is your own heart "in the house of mourning"?

For Thought and Discussion: Why is it hard for us to receive a rebuke — even from a wise person, as mentioned in 7:5?

For Thought and Discussion: In what ways might some of today's popular music be likened to "the song of fools" in 7:5?

Optional Application: In what situations in life have you needed "the rebuke of a wise person" (7:5)? And how can you continue to heed that wise counsel?

7:5-6 _____

7:8a _____

7:8b-9 _____

2. With 7:2-4 in mind, describe what you see as the lasting benefit to being "in the house of mourning."

3. How would you reconcile the teaching of 7:2-4 with the kind of joy and gladness that was commended earlier in Ecclesiastes 5:20?

4. Reflect on the first statement in 7:8. In what practical ways is it good to remember this truth?

_____

_____

_____

5. Consider carefully the final statement in 7:8. In what common ways do patience and pride often clash?

_____

_____

_____

6. How have you recognized the foolishness of anger, as mentioned in 7:9?

_____

_____

_____

_____

7. Reflect on 7:10. Why do you think it is unwise to think that "the old days" were any better than the present?

_____

_____

_____

_____

"Wise people certainly learn from the past, but they live in the present with all its opportunities. Overmuch dwelling on the past can prevent us from overcoming the world, which often seems so much more wicked today than ever before."[1]

Optional Application: Because "the end of a matter is better than its beginning" (7:8), what important things have you begun that need to be brought to completion?

Optional Application: In what aspects or situations of your life is it especially important for you to demonstrate the kind of patience mentioned in 7:8?

For Further Study: With Ecclesiastes 7:9 in mind regarding the foolishness of anger, what confirming teaching do you find in Proverbs 14:17; 16:32; Matthew 5:22; Ephesians 4:31; 2 Timothy 2:24-25; James 1:19-20?

For Thought and Discussion: With the truth of 7:10 in mind, how can we best learn from the past while still avoiding the unwise mind-set that the past was any better than the present?

For Further Study:
Ecclesiastes 7:12 tells us that wisdom preserves life. How do you see this further taught in Job 22:21-25; Proverbs 2:7-11; 3:18; 8:35; 9:11; 13:20; Isaiah 33:6?

8. Explain in your own words the benefit of wisdom as expressed in 7:11-12.

_____

_____

_____

_____

Wisdom is a shelter as money is a shelter (7:12). "Literally the phrase is 'In the shade is wisdom, in the shade is money' ('shade' in eastern thought represented *protection*). In other words, with wisdom and money, you've got it made in the shade!"[2]

9. a. What are we taught about God in 7:13-14?

_____

_____

_____

_____

b. What are we taught in 7:13-14 about mankind?

_____

_____

_____

_____

What God . . . has made crooked (7:13). This "does not make a moral judgment on God (see 1:15). It is meant to stress his sovereign control over all events."[3]

10. In what ways have you observed the same things that the author of Ecclesiastes mentions in 7:15?

_____

_____

_____

_____

**Optional
Application:** In the
current circumstances
of your life, would
you say that "times
are good" or "times
are bad" (7:14)? Either
way, what helps you
to see that God is
in control of your
circumstances?

"There are some things that we cannot alter, at least for the time being. This does not mean that we should not try to right wrongs and relive suffering; the Teacher frequently protests against those who permit oppression (e.g., verses 7-8). It is easy to blame God when things go wrong and to forget to thank him when good things come (verse 14). As children of God, we commonly experience both good and bad and may even thank God for allowing hardships rather than giving us an entirely smooth passage (see Matthew 8:20; Luke 10:38; 2 Corinthians 14-7). Part of the life of faith is accepting prosperity and adversity from God's hand without being able to explain just how everything will be worked out for the future (verse 14; Romans 8:28)."⁴

For Further Study:
How does the appar-
ent "balance" seen in
7:16-17 compare to
the practical truth
in the words of Jesus
in Matthew 5:20 and
23:27-28 and Luke
7:44-47?

11. How would you express in your own words what is being taught in 7:16-18?

_____

_____

_____

_____

For Further Study:
How would being "overrighteous" (7:16) compare with what Jesus warns against throughout Matthew 23? How were the scribes and Pharisees "overrighteous"? (See also Matthew 5:20.)

"Some interpret this passage [7:16-17] as giving them the right to establish their own standards and rules in their own minds for living life. They do this based on the notion that these verses are teaching that there is danger in having too much substance to one's religious practices. In reality, however, God examines the heart of the individual and knows the motives behind one's actions (Hebrews 4:12). God alone knows whether a person is practicing religion in form only, or if he is sincere."[5]

"We're creatures of extremes: 'If I'm going to be good, I'm going to be *good* at being good'—we fall so easily into a trap. . . . 'Why ruin yourself?' Solomon says. Why get a spiritual hernia? Your pursuit of righteousness just may destroy the very character of true righteousness. Your pursuit of being good is the very thing that will create trouble with your arrogance.

"Where does an honest godliness come in? Here's the balance: I know I'm a sinner who has been forgiven by God because of what Jesus Christ did on the cross for me. Because I am forgiven, that love and grace motivate me to pursue pleasing God. My goal is *not* to be good or righteous, but *to be pleasing to Him*. . . .

"We try so hard to be good. Why not just please Him, and let Him take care of the good?"[6]

12. Reflect on 7:19. In what ways have you observed wisdom's connection with power and strength?

_____

_____

_____

_____

For Further Study:
How does the thought of not being "overwicked" (Ecclesiastes 7:17) compare with New Testament teaching in Romans 6:6-13; Galatians 6:7-8; 1 John 1:8?

"Wisdom is not the knowledge of accumulated facts but the inner strength that comes from a God-instructed conscience. Hence we see the link between the fear of God (verse 18) and the true wisdom that gives inner strength (verse 10; see Proverbs 9:10), which is here contrasted with mere power."[7]

For Further Study:
How would you compare the teaching of Ecclesiastes 7:20 with Psalms 130:3; 143:2; Proverbs 20:9; Isaiah 53:6; Romans 3:23; James 3:2; 1 John 1:8-10?

13. How was the truth of 7:20 altered by the coming of Christ Jesus to earth?

_____

_____

_____

_____

14. What reason is given in 7:22 for the advice given in verse 21? What larger truths might this imply about the condition of our hearts in general and how this should affect our conduct?

_____

_____

_____

_____

_____

"People bad-mouth each other—it's as certain as sin. Solomon's counsel is to choose to see it for what it is: a demonstration of the problem of sin."[8]

All this I tested by wisdom ... so I turned my mind to understand, to investigate and to search out wisdom and the scheme of things ... this is what I have discovered ... still searching ... this only have I found (7:23,25,27-29). His quest continues.

---

15. How would you summarize the search undertaken in 7:23-26 as well as its results?

_____

_____

_____

_____

Madness of folly (7:25). "This has a modern ring, chiming in with some of our attempts to bypass the rational by exploring the absurd and the world of hallucinations."[9] "Not only do we say dumb things, we also *do* dumb things—'folly and the folly of madness,' Solomon calls it (7:25). *Folly* speaks of being 'plump in the head,' sluggish ... stupid ... living in a stupor, dazed, dulled, not understanding. *Madness* speaks of being unable to use our minds because our emotions and drives have taken over."[10]

The woman who is a snare (7:26). "Verse 26 may reflect Solomon's experiences with his hundreds of wives and concubines (1 Kings 11:3-4). Though Solomon's desire to compete with other Oriental potentates may in large measure account for his building up a royal harem, he found that a harem did not provide the appropriate companion for man. How much better he would have been with one good wife, such as he speaks of in 9:9 and Proverbs 31!"[11] "Solomon is speaking of the dark side of woman, and how it is used to control a man. Why is Solomon picking on the women? Because he's a man. But the converse is true as well. Look again at Genesis 3:16. The dark side of man is to rule over the woman, to have her serve his sensual needs. Sexual seduction brings out the sin problem in both."[12]

Escape her (7:26). "The man who fears God wants to please God, and it will be seen in his sexual behavior; he will escape the seduction. The man who lives to please himself will not."[13]

For Further Study:
How does the teaching in Ecclesiastes 7:26 compare with what you see in Proverbs 5?

16. Summarize the discoveries mentioned in 7:27-29.

_____

_____

_____

_____

Not finding (7:28). The verse continues, "One man among a thousand I found, but a woman among all these I have not found" (ESV). The adjective "upright" (NIV) is not in the Hebrew original. Most likely the passage "is not about 'upright' men and women but about 'wise' men and women"; the author "found that an absolutely wise man is exceedingly rare, one in a thousand; but so far he had not found even this tiny percentage among women. One cannot blame God for this; so the fault lies in man's misuse of his freedom (verse 29)."[14] "This is probably more of a comment on the way he [Solomon] *approached* women than a comment on women. His wives and concubines were trying to please him, not God. Despite the Lord's warning, Solomon 'held fast' to his hundreds of women, and they 'turned his heart away after other gods' (1 Kings 11:1-4)."[15]

17. How do the things mentioned in 7:29 relate to the theme expressed in Ecclesiastes 1:1-3?

_____

_____

_____

_____

Many schemes (7:29). "Man was created to be wise and good, but our decisions have brought out our dark side of sin. The solution is also a decision we make, by God's grace provided in Christ: 'We beg you on behalf of Christ, be reconciled to God' (2 Corinthians 5:21)."[16]

"[The] fundamental conclusion to which Qohelet has come is that human beings generally . . . although created 'upright' by God, have gone astray. The precise manner of their straying, as described in verse 29, is significant: They have 'gone in search of many schemes.'" This same verb "is used in verses 25 and 28 ('search out,' 'searching') of Qohelet's own quest for comprehensive knowledge — that is, his own inquiry into the 'scheme of things' (verses 25,27). The language is deliberately chosen to suggest that Qohelet's quest is itself an indication of departure from God's ways. One of his individual findings, in fact, is that the larger attempt at finding wisdom is not only futile but sinful — an act of irreverence toward God (see verses 15-18)."[17]

18. What would you select as the key verse or passage in Ecclesiastes 7—one that best captures or reflects the dynamics of what this chapter is all about?

_____

_____

_____

_____

For Further Study: How is the statement in Ecclesiastes 7:29 that "God created mankind upright" confirmed in Genesis 1 and 2? And how are the "schemes" of Ecclesiastes 7:29 confirmed by Genesis 3 and Romans 5:12-14?

19. List any lingering questions you have about Ecclesiastes 7.

_____

_____

_____

_____

20. From what you've seen so far in this book, how would you summarize how the author of Ecclesiastes views the meaning of life?

_____

_____

_____

_____

For the Group

You may want to focus your discussion for lesson 5 especially on the following issues, themes, and concepts. Which of these are evident in Ecclesiastes 7, and how are they further developed there?

- The tragic reality of mankind's sinfulness
- The reality of our coming physical death
- Enjoying our work, and enjoying life's true pleasures as God's good gifts
- Recognizing life's frustrations and hardships
- The meaning of true wisdom

- Fearing God
- Gratefulness to God

The following numbered questions in lesson 5 may stimulate your best and most helpful discussion: 9, 10, 13, 16, 19, 20, and 21.

Remember to look also at the "For Thought and Discussion" questions in the margins.

1. J. Stafford Wright, *Ecclesiastes*, Expositor's Bible Commentary, vol. 5, ed. Frank E. Gabelein (Grand Rapids, MI: Zondervan, 1991), 1174.
2. Darryl DelHousaye, *Today for Eternity* (Sisters, OR: Questar, 1991), August 7.
3. Wright, 1175.
4. Wright, 1175.
5. Warren Baker, ed., *The Complete Word Study Old Testament* (Chattanooga, TN: AMG, 1994), on Ecclesiastes 7:16-17.
6. DelHousaye, September 13.
7. Wright, 1176.
8. DelHousaye, June 29.
9. Derek Kidner, *The Message of Ecclesiastes*, The Bible Speaks Today, ed. J. A. Motyer (Downers Grove, IL: Inter-Varsity, 1976), 17.
10. DelHousaye, June 29.
11. Wright, 1177–1178.
12. DelHousaye, June 27.
13. DelHousaye, June 27.
14. Wright, 1177.
15. DelHousaye, June 28.
16. DelHousaye, June 29.
17. Iain Provan, *Ecclesiastes/Song of Songs*, The NIV Application Commentary (Grand Rapids, MI: Zondervan, 2001), 154.

ECCLESIASTES 8–9

Living Well Before God

Ecclesiastes 8

1. How does the observation in 8:1 contrast with the mood in 7:25-29?

_____

_____

_____

_____

"Chapter 7 concluded with a pessimistic view of man's attainment of wisdom. . . . Here [in 8:1] the Teacher shakes himself out of his depression. There *are* true wise men; and while true wisdom must be realistic, it need not make a person perpetually gloomy."[1]

"No one has an edge on the man who has wisdom. He knows the art of life, and has the skill to live it. He has the 'interpretation,' the right understanding of how things around him fit into the scheme of his life, how they all — the good and the bad — have their needful place in his living. He has the right *perspective*.

"You can see the uniqueness of this guy by his face. Because he understands what's happening to him, there's illumination there, a peace, a joy. There's a nonfearing presence about him. He's actually cheerful, which will cause him to stand out from the crowd like a flagpole.

"That 'perspective' has changed his hard, 'stern' look to one of restfulness and contentment . . . because he knows the worth of wisdom."[2]

2. How would you summarize what is taught in 8:2-5 about the correct attitude toward a governing authority?

_____

_____

_____

_____

"It seems best to interpret 8:5-6 as exhorting the wise man at court, faced with a foolish ruler, to exercise patience rather than to give free reign to his true feelings — to remember that there is a time for everything, including divine judgment on foolishness and wickedness."[3]

3. How does 8:6 build upon, amplify, or reinforce the earlier message of Ecclesiastes 3:1-8?

_____

_____

_____

_____

For Further Study:
How does the truth of 8:8 compare with the truth we see in Hebrews 9:27?

4. What human limitations are highlighted in 8:6-9?

_____

_____

_____

No one has power over the time of their death
(8:8). "Only Christ was able to say that He had 'power to lay it (His life) down' and the 'power to take it again' (John 10:18)."[4]

The truths in Ecclesiastes 8:7-9 "are general ones that might apply to anyone, and in particular to the wise person, who may be tempted to think that he can change things by his words and actions that cannot in fact be changed for the moment (at this 'time')."[5]

All this I saw, as I applied my mind to everything . . . I applied my mind to know . . . and to observe . . . then I saw all (8:9,16-17). His quest continues.

---

5. What observations are made in 8:10-13 about the destiny of the wicked?

_____

_____

For Further Study:
How would you compare Ecclesiastes 8:12 with Proverbs 1:7?

For Thought and Discussion: How do the observations in Ecclesiastes 8:10-13 highlight mankind's need for the gospel of Jesus Christ?

"The servant of God knows that he lives in a fallen world, where bad men often escape punishment. Nevertheless, the servant of God looks for the enduring approval of his Lord, for this is the purpose of living (verse 12)."[6]

It will not go well . . . their days will not lengthen (8:13). "Living a long time is not necessarily the same as prolonging one's days—a concept made meaningful by the revelation of eternal life in Christ. Such life is both qualitatively and quantitatively beyond any number of years on earth. The Teacher obviously believes in a future judgment (11:9). The day of the wicked, however long it lasts, will not be the normal day that closes with the lengthening of the evening shadows (verse 13)."[7]

"The wicked may sin massively—a hundred times over—and yet live a long life. This is admittedly puzzling if God is good and just and truly governs the universe. Yet Qohelet resists the conclusion that wickedness pays. He continues to affirm that it will go better with the person who fears God than with the person who does not (8:12-13), and he explicitly states that the days of the wicked 'will not lengthen like a shadow,' by which is probably meant that the life of the wicked is a fleeting and insubstantial thing that does not last long."[8]

6. How does 8:14 build upon, amplify, or reinforce the earlier message of Ecclesiastes 7:15?

_____

_____

_____

_____

_____

For Further Study:
How is the message of 8:14 further clarified and expanded in Malachi 3:13–4:3?

For Further Study:
How does the message of Ecclesiastes 8:15 compare with the words of Jesus in Matthew 6:25-34?

7. How does 8:15 build upon, amplify, or reinforce the earlier message of Ecclesiastes 2:24-25?

_____

_____

_____

_____

_____

"The more capacity one has for thinking things out, the more one is puzzled by the apparent meaninglessness of life. So man must be content to take the pieces one by one, without being able to fit them (past, present, and future) into the plan that he knows must be there (3:11)."[9]

8. What human limitations are highlighted in 8:16-17?

_____

_____

_____

_____

_____

The author of Ecclesiastes "expresses his confidence in the moral nature of the universe while noting various data that bring this intoapparent question. Unable finally to resolve the puzzle himself, he then characteristically advocates that the reader get on with life and not worry too much about the details, which lie with God.

"That is precisely the direction in which he moves in verses 15-17 (of Ecclesiastes 8). If it is ultimately unclear how justice is to be achieved and precisely how, in the longer term, it is 'better' to fear God than not to, then at least this much is clear: There is nothing 'better' for someone living in the present time 'under the sun' than to eat, drink and be glad — to know joy in the presence of God in his world. The business of living well before God in this way must not be sacrificed in the pursuit of truth that is ultimately beyond our grasp."[10]

No one can comprehend (8:17). "All efforts at knowing wisdom, in the sense of 'finding' a comprehensive account of reality, have failed. A more literal translation of part of verse 17 communicates the emphasis with which the failure is announced: 'NO human being can find out the work that is done under the sun. Despite all human efforts to search it out, one cannot find it. Even if the wise man claims to know, he cannot find it.' It is this reality that leads to the advice of verse 15 ['I commend the enjoyment of life . . .']. It is not the ultimate justice of God that Qohelet doubts. It is his own ability to understand how that justice works out in practice. He does not consider it wise to pursue that question at the expense of living well the life God has given him."[11]

9. What would you select as the key verse or passage in Ecclesiastes 8—one that best captures or reflects the dynamics of what this chapter is all about?

_____

_____

_____

_____

For Thought and Discussion: What does it mean to be "in God's hands" (9:1)? What difference would it make to *not* be in God's hands?

10. List any lingering questions you have about Ecclesiastes 8.

_____

_____

_____

_____

Ecclesiastes 9

11. What universal factors in human experience are emphasized in 9:1-3?

_____

_____

_____

_____

"When trouble comes, it is easy to ask, 'What have I done to deserve this?' It is less easy to ask the same question when happiness comes."[12]

12. How would you express in your own words the main point in 9:4-6?

_____

_____

_____

_____

"The Teacher . . . is leading up to the way we ought to live in view of the finality of death. Instead of living the rotten life of drifting self-indulgence (verse 3), we should ask the further question, 'What is the real purpose of life?' While there is life, there is hope — but hope for what? Surely, in the light of this book, there is hope for using life to the full. A dog that is alive can respond in a way that is impossible for the king of beasts when he is dead (verse 4)."[13]

The dead know nothing (9:5). "The Teacher believes in a future judgment (12:14); so here he cannot be teaching the nonexistence of the departed. . . . The Teacher is not teaching soul-sleep here, that the dead have no consciousness. Rather his emphasis is on the contrast between the carnal knowledge of the living and the dead."[14]

13. Here in chapter 9, how do verses 4, 6, and 10 build upon, amplify, or reinforce the earlier message of Ecclesiastes 3:19-21?

_____

_____

_____

_____

14. In your perspective, how thoroughly accurate is the statement made in 9:5 about "the living"?

_____

_____

_____

_____

15. How does 9:7-9 build upon, amplify, or reinforce the earlier message of Ecclesiastes 2:24; 3:12-13; 5:18-20; 8:15?

_____

_____

_____

_____

God has already approved what you do [NIV, ESV; "God has already accepted your works," NKJV] (9:7).

16. How would you explain God's "favor" that is mentioned in 9:7? What does it include, and what is the reason for it?

_____

_____

_____

_____

_____

_____

17. How would you express in your own words the teaching in 9:10?

_____

_____

_____

_____

The words of Ecclesiastes 9:10 provide us with "a ruling principle which should govern one's accomplishments in this life. Goals should be

(continued on page 92)

For Further Study: Read Psalm 16:8-11; Isaiah 25:7-8; 26:19; Daniel 12:2-3. See also Peter's explanation of Psalm 16:8-11 in Acts 2:22-36. What do these Old Testament passages teach about a future resurrection?

Optional Application: How fully do you actually *enjoy* your life? Do you enjoy it to the degree that we're taught to enjoy it in Ecclesiastes (as in 9:7-9)? If not, why not?

For Further Study:
How does the
message of 9:10
compare with the
words of Jesus in
John 9:4? How does
it compare also with
what you see in
Romans 12:11;
1 Corinthians 10:31;
2 Corinthians 5:10;
Colossians 3:5-14?

(continued from page 91)
fervor and energy that one can display. In doing
so, it should be understood that there are
limits given to what is meant by the phrase
'whatever thy hand findeth to do.' People need
to use wisdom in determining which goals
are within their capabilities. . . . The focus of
this verse in Ecclesiastes is on the attitude of
the heart, or better the motives behind the
actions. Solomon wrote, 'do it with thy might.'
This word 'might' is also used to describe how
one's worship for God should be conducted:
'Love the Lord thy God . . . with all thy might'
(Deuteronomy 6:5). God's desire is for
obedience, but He also requires that it be done
from a pure heart."[15]

18. Notice the four aspects of life mentioned at the
end of 9:10 as arenas for intense involvement
("with all your might"). What particular significance do you see in each of these four?

"working"

"planning"

"knowledge"

_____

_____

"wisdom"

_____

_____

_____

_____

"Be devoted to life. Learn that God is good by enjoying the good He's given you. Then you'll be able to trust Him in the darkest times.

"And be devoted to the Author of life! Give Him thanks continually for His good gifts.

"Now's the time to get on with it — with life! Enjoy life by _doing the significant_ — by doing what's important with your life. Work hard at it! As Jim Elliot said, 'Wherever you are, be all there!' ...

"The time to do the significant for God is _now_ — on this side of the grave. ...

"If you're elderly, I urge you especially to think about this. Of all people, you should be the first to be working for the Lord, not the last. If your days on earth are coming to an end, don't go on vacation now."[16]

"Solomon's conclusion that death makes vain all human labor and wisdom on earth ('under the sun'; 1:14,17; 2:11,17) does not mean that people should

Optional Application: In your life, what are the most important things that fit in the category of "whatever your hand finds to do" (9:10)? To what degree are you doing these things "with all your might"? In what areas is there a need for you to be more intense, more wholehearted, and harder working?

abandon society and culture to lead an ascetic life. Neither does the Christian priority of proclaiming the gospel for the conversion of sinners (a 'labor . . . not in vain,' 1 Corinthians 15:58) mean Christians should abdicate their cultural responsibilities.

"On the contrary, Solomon commands (9:7-10) God's people to enjoy life, despite its futility, harsh realities, and uncertainties, and to work with full vigor. This practical approach to life is neither a version of Greek stoicism nor a product of human effort: it is a gift of God (3:13; 5:19) for those who fear Him and keep His commands (5:1-7; 12:13,14). Ecclesiastes teaches both the human responsibility to obey God joyfully, and God's sovereign provision of the ability to obey."[17]

So I reflected on all this . . . I have seen something else . . . I also saw (9:1,11,13). His quest continues.

---

19. Express in your own words the important reminders we're given in 9:11-12.

_____

_____

_____

_____

"These five assets [in Ecclesiastes 9:11] appear to be everything you would need to guarantee success: 'the swift' are those who are quick to see and grab opportunities; 'the warriors' are the strong, the tough, the competitive; 'the wise' have good sense; 'the discerning' are the shrewd, the meticulous; and 'men of ability' are those trained and educated. But these human abilities do not guarantee success. Ultimately, success or failure depends on something else."[18]

Chance (9:11). "The concept of chance in verse 11 is not exactly the English usage. It contains less the idea of haphazard occurrence than an event that we meet, whether anticipated or unanticipated."[19] "Time and chance are paired [in Ecclesiastes 9:11] because they have a way of taking matters suddenly out of our hands. God permits the good and bad to happen in our lives—but He is more interested in our responses to them than He is in the events themselves. He knows He can take *any* event that occurs and still produce good out of it."[20]

"It may seem strange that the Teacher can maintain faith in God's plan while accepting the factor of chance. His theme, however, is that we live in a world where we cannot calculate the future precisely but must share the day-by-day events that come to good and bad alike."[22]

"Qohelet does not yet express a *fully* Christian faith, of course. . . . Yet Qohelet's faith is *truly* Christian faith in its insistence that God is God and we are not, that God's ways in the world are beyond us and

Optional Application: Reflect well on Ecclesiastes 9:11 and what it says about your pursuits in life. "The issue, then, is this: When you fall down, what do you fall back on? When you've done all you can do, followed every success formula, and it still doesn't come off—what do you do?"[21] How would you personally answer that question?

For Further Study: How does the message of 9:11-12 compare with the words of Jesus in Matthew 5:45 about sunshine and rain?

beyond our control, that believers live the same human life as anyone else, and that they encounter the same range of human experiences even while God is present in their midst. He reminds us that 'biblical faith . . . is the radical abandonment of our whole being in grateful trust and love to . . . God,' not something we practice out of self-interest."[23]

20. Summarize what happens in the brief story that's told in 9:13-16. What point does the author of Ecclesiastes make in telling this story?

_____

_____

_____

_____

"The parable [in 9:13-16] is not a moral tale to show what people should do: it is a cautionary tale to show what they are like."[24]

21. a. How is wisdom further commended in 9:17-18?

_____

_____

_____

b. How do these verses relate to the story told in 9:13-16?

_____

_____

_____

22. What would you select as the key verse or passage in Ecclesiastes 9 — one that best captures or reflects the dynamics of what this chapter is all about?

_____

_____

_____

_____

_____

23. List any lingering questions you have about Ecclesiastes 9.

_____

_____

_____

_____

_____

For the Group

You may want to focus your discussion for lesson 6 especially on the following issues, themes, and concepts. Which of these are evident in Ecclesiastes 8 and 9, and how are they further developed there?

- The tragic reality of mankind's sinfulness
- The reality of our coming physical death
- Enjoying our work, and enjoying life's true pleasures as God's good gifts
- Recognizing life's frustrations and hardships
- The meaning of true wisdom
- Fearing God
- Gratefulness to God

The following numbered questions in lesson 6 may stimulate your best and most helpful discussion: 1, 2, 5, 8, 9, 10, 11, 16, 17, 19, 22, and 23.

Remember to look also at the "For Thought and Discussion" questions in the margins.

1. J. Stafford Wright, *Ecclesiastes*, Expositor's Bible Commentary, vol. 5, ed. Frank E. Gabelein (Grand Rapids, MI: Zondervan, 1991), 1178.
2. Darryl DelHousaye, *Today for Eternity* (Sisters, OR: Questar, 1991), August 7.
3. Iain Provan, *Ecclesiastes/Song of Songs*, The NIV Application Commentary (Grand Rapids, MI: Zondervan, 2001), 166.
4. Warren Baker, ed., *The Complete Word Study Old Testament* (Chattanooga, TN: AMG, 1994), on Ecclesiastes 8:8.
5. Provan, 166.
6. Wright, 1179.
7. Wright, 1179.
8. Provan, 167.
9. Wright, 1181.
10. Provan, 168.
11. Provan, 168.
12. Wright, 1181.
13. Wright, 1181.
14. Wright, 1181–1182.
15. Baker, on Ecclesiastes 9:10.
16. DelHousaye, October 21.
17. *New Geneva Study Bible* (Nashville: Thomas Nelson, 1995), introduction to Ecclesiastes, "Characteristics and Themes."
18. DelHousaye, October 30.
19. Wright, 1183.
20. DelHousaye, October 30.
21. DelHousaye, October 30.
22. Wright, 1183.
23. Provan, 185, quoting V. Ramachandra, *Gods That Fail: Modern Idolatry and Christian Mission* (Carlisle, PA: Paternoster, 1996), 40–42.
24. Derek Kidner, *The Message of Ecclesiastes*, The Bible Speaks Today, ed. J. A. Motyer (Downers Grove, IL: InterVarsity, 1976), 85.

ECCLESIASTES 10:1–11:6

Wisdom and Foolishness

Ecclesiastes 10

1. How is the spoiling influence of foolishness communicated in 10:1? How can being aware of this help us to live more wisely?

_____

_____

_____

_____

Right . . . left (10:2). These are "natural symbols for the strong and good, on the one hand, and for the weak and bad, on the other hand. The Latin word *sinister* means 'left,' but it also has the unpleasant metaphorical meaning that it has in English."[1]

2. What is implied in 10:2 about the stark difference in effect between wisdom and righteousness? How can being aware of this help us live more wisely?

For Thought and Discussion: Is foolishness normally as obvious as 10:3 would seem to suggest? What do you think?

For Further Study: How would you compare Ecclesiastes 10:3 with Proverbs 13:16?

Optional Application: In what kinds of situations are you tempted to lose your temper instead of responding with the kind of calmness that is commended in Ecclesiastes 10:4?

_____

_____

_____

_____

_____

_____

3. How is the obvious inferiority of foolishness communicated in 10:3?

_____

_____

_____

_____

4. According to 10:4, why is it important to react calmly to a negative encounter with anyone who is your superior in some way?

_____

_____

_____

_____

5. In what ways have you observed the same kinds of realities that are mentioned in 10:5-7?

_____

_____

_____

_____

6. Reflect carefully on the illustrations given in 10:8-11. What message can be found there to help us in facing risks and hardships?

_____

_____

_____

_____

Stones . . . logs (10:9). "You need stones and wood for building; then make sure that a boulder does not fall on you or a piece of wood fly in your face."[2]

Are gracious ["win him favor," ESV] (10:12). "Sensible talk meets with approval."[3] See Luke 4:22. This favor or grace "springs from the basic humility which is the beginning of wisdom."[4]

7. What realities about foolish talk are highlighted in 10:12-14?

_____

_____

_____

_____

No one knows what is coming (10:14). This fact "does not prevent a fool from multiplying words about it . . . making many groundless predictions."[5]

8. What reality about foolishness is emphasized in 10:15?

_____

_____

_____

_____

Toil of fools (10:15). "In the context, 'work' may relate to the many arguments of verse 14. . . . A person may be so involved in arguing about

For Thought and Discussion: With 10:8-9 in mind, how much true risk and danger do we typically face in our lives today? And what do you see as the benefits (if any) for taking such risks?

Optional Application: Think about any important situations in your life where you are facing risk, hardship, danger, or a need for effective planning (or maybe all those things!). As you face any of these, what practical help can you find in 10:8-11 for the right actions or attitudes?

For Further Study: How does the teaching in 10:12-14 about wisdom and foolishness compare with the New Testament teaching in 1 Corinthians 1:18-25 and in Matthew 7:24-27? What are the connections?

the universe that he misses what the ordinary person is concerned about, namely, finding the way home (see Isaiah 35:8-10)."[6]

9. What principles for effective leadership are taught in 10:16-17?

_____

_____

_____

_____

A servant ["a child," ESV, NKJV] (10:16). "The word certainly designates an inexperienced person in this context. . . . Those under the influence of such leaders get no benefit from them."[7]

10. What commonsense principle is taught in 10:18?

_____

_____

_____

11. What helpful perspectives do you see in 10:19 for how we should live?

_____

_____

_____

_____

12. What practical warning is highlighted for us in 10:20?

_____

_____

_____

Ecclesiastes 10:20 "is a warning that malice toward the powers that be may lead to ultimate confrontation with them. If there is something wrong in your town or in the place where you work, you must either keep totally silent or be prepared for your proper criticisms to come to the ears of those at the top."[8]

Ecclesiastes 11:1-6

"At last the Teacher is approaching the climax of his book. We cannot see God's whole plan, and there is nothing in this world that we can build on so as to find satisfaction or the key to the meaning of things. Yet we are to fulfill God's purpose by accepting our daily lot in life as from him and by thus pleasing him make each day a good day. But how can we please him where there is so much we cannot understand?

"The Teacher has already shown that certain things stand out as right or wrong, and a sensible conscience will see these as an indication of what God desires. This section [Ecclesiastes 11:1-6] gives further wise advice in the light of an uncertain future. We must use common sense in sensible planning and in eliminating as many of the uncertainties as we can. . . .

"We must recognize the certainties but must plan in such a way as not to be thrown off balance when the unexpected happens."[9]

13. How does 11:1-2 imply the appropriateness of diversification in financial investment or in charitable giving? What reasons are given for this?

_____

_____

_____

_____

_____

14. What other observations of the natural world could communicate essentially the same thing as what 11:3 is speaking of?

_____

_____

_____

15. If verse 3 refers to stormy conditions (with the tree being blown over by wind), does verse 4 represent appropriate caution or foolish delay in the task at hand? Explain your answer.

_____

_____

_____

_____

As you do not know the path of the wind, or how the body is formed in a mother's womb ["As you do not know the way the spirit comes to the bones in the womb of a woman with child," ESV] (11:5). "It is likely that Jesus Christ had this verse in mind when he told Nicodemus, 'The wind blows wherever it pleases. You hear its sound, but you cannot tell where it comes from or where it is going' (John 3:8). . . . The Greek word (*pneuma*) also can have either meaning, and some translate Christ's words as 'The spirit breathes where he will.'"[10]

16. What do you see as the significance of the statement in 11:5?

_____

_____

_____

_____

17. What reason for diligent work is given in 11:6?

_____

_____

_____

_____

18. How do verses 1-6 in chapter 11 reflect the fact that life is unpredictable, and why is this important to properly recognize?

_____

_____

_____

_____

_____

19. What would you select as the key verse or passage in Ecclesiastes 10:1–11:6 — one that best captures or reflects the dynamics of what this section of Ecclesiastes is all about?

_____

_____

_____

20. List any lingering questions you have about this section of Ecclesiastes (10:1–11:6).

_____

_____

For Thought and Discussion: Reflect on Ecclesiastes 11:5. How much does God *want* us to understand about how He works? To what degree are we able to understand this?

Optional Application: In what God-given tasks is it especially important for you now to stay busy, morning and evening (see 11:6)?

_____

_____

For the Group

You may want to focus your discussion for lesson 7 especially on the following issues, themes, and concepts. Which of these are evident in Ecclesiastes 10:1–11:6, and how are they further developed there?

- The tragic reality of mankind's sinfulness
- The reality of our coming physical death
- Enjoying our work, and enjoying life's true pleasures as God's good gifts
- Recognizing life's frustrations and hardships
- The meaning of true wisdom
- Fearing God
- Gratefulness to God

The following numbered questions in lesson 7 may stimulate your best and most helpful discussion: 1, 2, 4, 5, 6, 10, 11, 16, 17, 18, 19, and 20.

And again, remember to look at the "For Thought and Discussion" questions in the margins.

1. J. Stafford Wright, *Ecclesiastes*, Expositor's Bible Commentary, vol. 5, ed. Frank E. Gabelein (Grand Rapids, MI: Zondervan, 1991), 1185.
2. Wright, 1186.
3. Wright, 1187.
4. Derek Kidner, *The Message of Ecclesiastes*, The Bible Speaks Today, ed. J. A. Motyer (Downers Grove, IL: InterVarsity, 1976), 92.
5. *ESV Study Bible* (Wheaton, IL: Crossway, 2008), on Ecclesiastes 10:14.
6. Wright, 1187.
7. Wright, 1187.
8. Wright, 1188.
9. Wright, 1188–1190.
10. Wright, 1190.

ECCLESIASTES 11:7–12:14

Reality Proclaimed

Ecclesiastes 11:7-10

> The theme of youth and contrasting old age is introduced in 11:7-10 and will continue through much of Ecclesiastes 12.

1. What observations about youth are made in 11:7-10?

_____

_____

_____

_____

Days of darkness (11:8). "It is usual to refer 'the days of darkness' only to death. . . . But there is no real reason to include death at all, in view of the use of darkness to describe the effects of old age in 12:2-3."[1]

While you are young (11:9). "The young man has vitality at its fullest; and if he cannot feel the sense of fulfillment in it, something is wrong."[2]

For Further Study:
How does the message of 11:9-10 compare with New Testament teaching in 2 Corinthians 5:10; 7:1; Colossians 3:5-14?

For all these things (11:9). God's good gifts are to be fully and appropriately enjoyed, always with a sense of gratitude and responsibility before Him. "Rab, a Jewish teacher of the third century A.D., commented, 'Man will have to give account for all that he saw and did not enjoy.'"[3]

2. How would you explain in your own words the counsel given in 11:10?

_____

_____

_____

_____

3. How does this part of chapter 11 build upon, amplify, or reinforce the earlier message of Ecclesiastes 3:21 and 9:4-10?

_____

_____

_____

_____

"Reality must be proclaimed, especially since many of our young people today, unlike most of their predecessors throughout history, gain little direct experience of death even through their family experience. They have little contact with the dead, even when it is a relative, and little experience of nursing the dying. It is all too easy, therefore, for mortality never to have stared them in the face and to have challenged them about their identity and value.

"The young person also needs to be told, however, about the goodness of God and to be encouraged to live responsively to that goodness. This involves virtue, of course, but it also involves joy. It is important to speak about both."[4]

For Thought and Discussion: What do you see as the most important elements in a healthy and realistic expectation of old age and death?

Ecclesiastes 12

4. Chapter 12 has been called the key to the book of Ecclesiastes. Why might this be so?

_____

_____

_____

_____

Remember your Creator (12:1). "The use of the term 'Creator' reveals that a person owes a great debt to the One who has formed him. How can he do less than serve and devote his life to God? When this fact is realized, then one can reflect on his life with peace in his heart."[5]

In 12:1-8, "whatever the interpretation of phrases, the whole picture of decrepit old age is conveyed clearly."[6]

5. How does 12:1-8 build upon, amplify, or reinforce the earlier message of Ecclesiastes 11:7-10?

_____

_____

_____

_____

Almond tree blossoms (12:5). "The almond tree pictures the white hair of age. To us it is usually the harbinger of spring, and the blossom is pink. In Palestine, however, the tree begins to blossom in midwinter; and although the petals are pink at their base, they are white towards the tip. The general impression of the tree in flower is of a white mass."[7]

Before (12:6). This word recalls 12:1: "before the days of trouble come."

Bowl . . . pitcher . . . well (12:6). "The common link between most of the images used in verse 6 appears to be that they are water receptacles; since water is a symbol of life (2 Samuel 14:14; John 4:14; Revelation 21:6; 22:1,17), the destruction of these various items indicates the moment when mortal life ceases."[8] "The pictures in this verse have met with a variety of interpretations, but they certainly describe total collapse."[9]

"This [the wording of 12:2-7] is the language of the unmaking of creation. . . . For every person is in the end 'unmade.' It is forceful language with which to address the young man, who is thus confronted with the unmaking of creation as his inevitable future, so that he may take seriously the exhortation to remember his Creator in the present."[10]

6. How would you describe and explain the effectiveness of the images given in 12:2-7 of physical decline and death?

_____

_____

_____

"The Old Testament consistently teaches that at death the life principle in humans and animals alike (Ecclesiastes 3:19-21; Psalm 104:29-30) returns to God, the Giver of life, and that we must one day give account to God (Ecclesiastes 11:9)."[11]

7. What is the full meaning of the statement in 12:8?

_____

_____

_____

_____

"Remembering one's Creator in the time of one's youth . . . is shown to be especially important in view of the gradual loss of vitality as age takes its toll of the body and brain. Old age and death are the supreme frustration and vanity that we experience. We naturally wonder what the aging process would have been if we had not fallen. The Transfiguration [Matthew 17:2; Mark 9:2-3; Luke 9:29-31] probably indicates what would have happened. Jesus Christ, being without sin, had the opportunity of receiving a transformation of his ordinary body and of passing to heaven without dying. Instead of this, he deliberately chose to go forward and die for the sins of mankind. . . .

"As we grow older, we all have some traces of these marks of age, even if they

For Further Study: Ecclesiastes 12:7 speaks of the time for each of us when "the dust returns to the ground it came from, and the spirit returns to God who gave it." "The belief in an afterlife has always been a part of God's revealed faith."[12] Study how that truth is revealed in the following Old Testament passages: Genesis 5:24; 2 Samuel 12:23; Job 19:25; Psalms 17:15; 49:15; 73:24,26.

do not develop to the extremes that this chapter describes. So the Teacher is justified in reminding young people that they cannot afford to put off faith in God their Creator until they are older. God wants the best of their lives."[13]

"Meaningless! Meaningless!" says the Teacher. "Everything is meaningless!" (12:8). "A better translation is this: 'Fleeting, fleeting,' says Qohelet, 'everything is fleeting.'"[14]

---

8. What do you see as the most important accomplishments mentioned in 12:9-10?

_____

_____

_____

_____

"The author tells us [in 12:9-10] exactly how he went about his task, and in the same passage provides his self-characterization: he is a teacher, a collector and careful arranger of proverbs, a stylist and wordsmith, and a person in quest of the truth."[15]

"We have the portrait of a scholar whose vocation is teaching, research, editing, and creative writing. What his book as a whole tells us indirectly is that he is as sensitive as he is courageous, and a master of style."[16]

Not only was the Teacher wise (12:9). "Solomon . . .
in spite of personal failings, must have retained
the gift of wisdom, which he had asked for and
obtained for the benefit of his people (Ecclesiastes 2:9; see 1 Kings 3:9-12; 4:29-34)"; as
spoken by Solomon himself, the words in 12:9-12
would be "no more boastful than are the words
of the prophets who claim to be speaking the
words of the Lord."[17]

Goads (12:11). The words of the wise "help guide
one along the proper path. (A 'goad' is a long,
pointed stick used for prodding and guiding
oxen while plowing.)"[18] They are "sharp words
to prod us out of our haze, motivating us to
think right, to escape the stupor of simply sur-
viving."[19] "Wisdom must be allowed to do its
painful work on our lives, as the goads bite."[20]

Firmly embedded nails (12:11). "The words of
the wise provide moral and intellectual sta-
bility."[21] "His words are 'well-driven nails,'
words to hang something on or to fasten
something permanently—words to stand the
pressure of real life."[22]

One shepherd (12:11). See Genesis 48:15; 49:24;
Psalms 23:1; 28:9; 80:1; Ezekiel 34:23; 37:24;
John 10:11,16.

"Verse 11 claims God's inspiration for
the Wisdom writers and hence is very
important. It is their equivalent of 'Thus
saith the Lord.' . . . The wise draw their
wisdom from the Shepherd of Israel, the
one true God."[23]

"The words of Qohelet and the wise . . .
are not primarily designed for use in
pursuing our own literary and intellectual
ends. They are designed so that we may
live well before God, reverencing him

Optional Application: How should the teaching and warning in Ecclesiastes 12:11-12 be applied to *your* choices in reading material and other media intake?

and bearing always in mind that the universe is a moral place in which there is accountability for the way in which we spend our days."[24]

9. According to 12:11-12, why should we pay careful attention to "the words of the wise"?

_____

_____

_____

_____

10. What are the most important truths about God that you see in 12:11-14?

_____

_____

_____

_____

_____

Verse 12 includes "a warning against the vast amount of literature that is a waste of time for the reader who is really concerned to find the truth."[25]

11. How does 12:13 build upon, amplify, or reinforce the earlier message of Ecclesiastes 3:14, 5:7, and 7:18?

_____

_____

_____

_____

Duty of all mankind (12:13). "The literal Hebrew, 'This is (for) all mankind,' is the equivalent of 'This is what man is made for' or 'This is the whole duty of man.'"[26] "True, it is among other things his whole duty; but the Hebrew does not say so: it leaves this wholeness undefined. 'This,' as we might translate it, 'is all that there is to man'; but it is an 'all' which stands in utter contrast to the 'vanity' with which the book has been confronting us. Here at last we shall find reality, and find ourselves."[27]

12. a. What are the most important connections between the message of 12:13-14 and the message of the entire Bible?

_____

_____

_____

_____

b. In particular, how does the message of 12:13-14 link with the gospel of Jesus Christ?

_____

_____

_____

_____

Now all has been heard; here is the conclusion (12:13). The author's quest is completed.

"A good author usually summarizes the main points that he has been making when he comes to the end of his book. The summary here is especially important, since commentators have tried to interpret the book as the thoughts of a skeptic.

For Further Study:
Reflect well on the closing line in the book of Ecclesiastes. How do you see its message further developed in Matthew 12:36; 25:31-46; Luke 12:1-2; John 5:28-29; Romans 2:16; 14:10-12; 1 Corinthians 4:5; 2 Corinthians 5:10; Revelation 20:11-15?

"Obviously, the Teacher is sometimes skeptical; but God is real to him, and he believes that God has revealed his will to mankind. If God had not done so, man could not be held accountable for his actions (12:14). Thus, although he would like to know more of the total plan of God, man knows enough to be held responsible for what he does or fails to do. His life day by day is to be lived as in the sight of God, who has given him the opportunity to fulfill God's purpose for that day."[28]

Fear God (12:13). "*Fear God* is a call that puts us in our place, and all other fears, hopes, and admirations in their place."[29]

"Do you take God seriously?

"When you can't figure Him out, do you still fear Him? For either you will fear the Creator or fear the creation; it takes the greater fear to dispel the lesser fear.

"God is God, and we are not. Fear Him without terror; fear Him with honor and reverence. Fear Him — and do what He says.

"As it is with fear, so it is with faith: 'Faith, if it has no works, is dead' (James 1:17). . . .

"Do you take God seriously?

"If you do, you'll keep His commandments.

"And you'll take seriously what He said about Jesus. God Himself declared from heaven: 'This is My beloved Son, with whom I am well-pleased; *listen to Him!'* (Matthew 17:5).

"As I live the 'now' of my life, forgetting neither what I've learned from my past nor the hope of my future, I want to understand what I can so I can know what I need to know — and do it right."[30]

13. In your opinion, in what ways do the closing lines serve as an especially appropriate and important conclusion to the book of Ecclesiastes?

_____

_____

_____

_____

14. How does 12:14 build upon or amplify or reinforce the earlier message of Ecclesiastes 11:9?

_____

_____

_____

_____

Every deed into judgment (12:14). "It kills complacency to know that nothing goes unnoticed and unassessed, not even the things that we disguise from ourselves. But at the same time it transforms life. If God cares as much as this, nothing can be pointless."[31]

Optional Application: Which verses in Ecclesiastes would be most helpful for you to memorize so you have them always available in your mind and heart for the Holy Spirit to use?

> The truth of the final verse "colors all the teaching of Christ, to whom no detail on earth could be too small to matter in heaven — an idle word, the death of a sparrow, a cup of cold water, the repentance of one sinner."[32]

15. What would you select as the key verse or passage in this final section of Ecclesiastes (11:7–12:14) — one that best captures or reflects the dynamics of what these verses are all about?

_____

_____

_____

_____

16. List any lingering questions you have about Ecclesiastes 11:7–12:14.

_____

_____

_____

_____

Reviewing Ecclesiastes

17. In Isaiah 55:10-11, God reminds us that in the same way He sends rain and snow from the sky to water the earth and nurture life so also He sends His words to accomplish specific purposes. What would you suggest are God's primary purposes for the message of Ecclesiastes in the lives of His people today?

_____

_____

_____

_____

_____

_____

18. Recall the guidelines given for our thought life
    in Philippians 4:8 — "Whatever is true, whatever
    is noble, whatever is right, whatever is pure,
    whatever is lovely, whatever is admirable — if
    anything is excellent or praiseworthy — *think
    about such things*" (emphasis added). As
    you reflect on all you've read in the book of
    Ecclesiastes, what stands out to you as being
    particularly *true*, or *noble*, or *right*, or *pure*,
    or *lovely*, or *admirable*, or *excellent*, or *praise-
    worthy* — and therefore well worth thinking
    more about?

    _____

    _____

    _____

    _____

19. Considering that all of Scripture testifies ulti-
    mately of Christ, where does Jesus come most
    in focus for you in this book?

    _____

    _____

    _____

20. In your understanding, what are the strongest
    ways in which Ecclesiastes points us to man-
    kind's need for Jesus and what He accomplished
    in His death and resurrection?

    _____

    _____

    _____

21. In Romans 15:4, Paul reminds us that the Old
    Testament Scriptures can give us patience and
    perseverance on one hand as well as comfort

and encouragement on the other. In your own life, how do you see the book of Ecclesiastes living up to Paul's description? In what ways does it help meet your personal needs for both *perseverance* and *encouragement*?

_____

_____

_____

_____

_____

22. What four- to six-word title would you give to this book to best summarize its content and significance?

_____

_____

_____

23. When you get to heaven, if you ask God, "Why did You include this book in the Bible?" how do you think He might answer?

_____

_____

_____

_____

For the Group

You may want to focus your discussion for lesson 8 especially on the following issues, themes, and concepts. Which of these are evident in Ecclesiastes 11:7–12:14, and how are they further developed there?

- The tragic reality of mankind's sinfulness
- The reality of our coming physical death
- Enjoying our work, and enjoying life's true pleasures as God's good gifts
- Recognizing life's frustrations and hardships
- The meaning of true wisdom
- Fearing God
- Gratefulness to God

The following numbered questions in lesson 8 may stimulate your best and most helpful discussion: 1, 2, 4, 7, 9, 10, 12, 13, 15, and 18.

Allow enough discussion time to look back together and review all of Ecclesiastes as a whole. You can use the numbered questions 17–23 in this lesson to help you do that.

Once more, look also at the questions in the margins under the heading "For Thought and Discussion."

1. J. Stafford Wright, *Ecclesiastes*, Expositor's Bible Commentary, vol. 5, ed. Frank E. Gabelein (Grand Rapids, MI: Zondervan, 1991), 1191.
2. Wright, 1191.
3. Wright, 1191.
4. Iain Provan, *Ecclesiastes/Song of Songs*, The NIV Application Commentary (Grand Rapids, MI: Zondervan, 2001), 223.
5. Warren Baker, ed., *The Complete Word Study Old Testament* (Chattanooga, TN: AMG, 1994), on Ecclesiastes 12:1.
6. Wright, 1194.
7. Wright, 1193.
8. *ESV Study Bible* (Wheaton, IL: Crossway, 2008), on Ecclesiastes 12:2-7.
9. Wright, 1194.
10. Provan, 214.
11. Wright, 1194.
12. Baker, on Ecclesiastes 9:10.
13. Wright, 1192.
14. Provan, 219.
15. Leland Ryken and Philip Graham Ryken, eds., *The Literary Study Bible* (Wheaton, IL: Crossway, 2007), introduction to Ecclesiastes, "The Book at a Glance."
16. Derek Kidner, *The Message of Ecclesiastes*, The Bible Speaks Today, ed. J. A. Motyer (Downers Grove, IL: InterVarsity, 1976), 22.
17. Wright, 1195.
18. *ESV Study Bible*, on Ecclesiastes 12:11.

19. Darryl DelHousaye, *Today for Eternity* (Sisters, OR: Questar, 1991), January 19.
20. Provan, 231.
21. *ESV Study Bible*, on Ecclesiastes 12:11.
22. DelHousaye, January 19.
23. Wright, 1196.
24. Provan, 228–229.
25. Wright, 1196.
26. Wright, 1197.
27. Kidner, 107.
28. Wright, 1197.
29. Kidner, 107.
30. DelHousaye, December 28.
31. Kidner, 107.
32. Kidner, 107.

STUDY AIDS

For further information on the material in this study, consider the following sources. They are available on the Internet (www.christianbook.com, www.amazon.com, etc.), or your local Christian bookstore should be able to order any of them if it does not carry them. Most seminary libraries have them, as well as many university and public libraries. If they are out of print, you might be able to find them online.

Commentaries on Ecclesiastes

Bridges, Charles, *An Exposition of the Book of Ecclesiastes* (Banner of Truth Trust, 1960).

Crenshaw, James L., *Ecclesiastes: A Commentary*, The Old Testament Library (Westminster, 1987).

Delitzsch, Franz, *Commentary on the Song of Songs and Ecclesiastes*, trans. M. G. Easton (Eerdmans, 1950).

Eaton, Michael A., *Ecclesiastes: An Introduction and Commentary*, Tyndale Old Testament Commentary, vol. 16 (InterVarsity, 1983).

Fox, Michael V., *A Time to Tear Down and a Time to Build Up: A Rereading of Ecclesiastes* (Eerdmans, 1999).

Hubbard, David A., *Ecclesiastes, Song of Solomon*, Mastering the Old Testament, vol. 15B (Word, 1991).

Kidner, Derek, *The Message of Ecclesiastes*, The Bible Speaks Today, ed. J. A. Motyer (InterVarsity, 1976).

Longman III, Tremper, *The Book of Ecclesiastes*, New International Commentary on the Old Testament (Eerdmans, 1998).

Murphy, Roland E., *Ecclesiastes*, Word Biblical Commentary, vol. 23A (Word, 1992).

Provan, Iain, *Ecclesiastes/Song of Songs*, The NIV Application Commentary (Zondervan, 2001).

Whybray, R. N., *Ecclesiastes*, The New Century Bible Commentary (Eerdmans, 1989).

Wright, J. Stafford, *Ecclesiastes*, Expositor's Bible Commentary, vol. 5 (Zondervan, 1991).

Historical Background Sources and Handbooks

Bible study becomes more meaningful when modern Western readers understand the times and places in which the biblical authors lived. *The IVP Bible Background Commentary: Old Testament*, by John H. Walton, Victor H. Matthews, and Mark Chavalas (InterVarsity, 2000), provides insight into the ancient Near Eastern world, its peoples, customs, and geography to help contemporary readers better understand the context in which the Old Testament Scriptures were written.

A **handbook** of biblical customs can also be useful. Some good ones are the time-proven updated classic *Halley's Bible Handbook with the New International Version*, by Henry H. Halley (Zondervan, 2007), and the inexpensive paperback *Manners and Customs in the Bible*, by Victor H. Matthews (Hendrickson, 1991).

Concordances, Dictionaries, and Encyclopedias

A **concordance** lists words of the Bible alphabetically along with each verse in which the word appears. It lets you do your own word studies. An *exhaustive* concordance lists every word used in a given translation, while an *abridged* or *complete* concordance omits either some words, some occurrences of the word, or both.

Two of the best exhaustive concordances are *Strong's Exhaustive Concordance* and *The Strongest NIV Exhaustive Concordance*. *Strong's* is available based on the King James Version of the Bible and the New American Standard Bible. *Strong's* has an index by which you can find out which Greek or Hebrew word is used in a given English verse. The NIV concordance does the same thing except it also includes an index for Aramaic words in the original texts from which the NIV was translated. However, neither concordance requires knowledge of the original languages. *Strong's* is available online at www.biblestudytools.com. Both are also available in hard copy.

A **Bible dictionary** or **Bible encyclopedia** alphabetically lists articles about people, places, doctrines, important words, customs, and geography of the Bible.

Holman Illustrated Bible Dictionary, by C. Brand, C. W. Draper, and A. England (B&H, 2003), offers more than seven hundred color photos, illustrations, and charts; sixty full-color maps; and up-to-date archeological findings, along with exhaustive definitions of people, places, things, and events—dealing with every subject in the Bible. It uses a variety of Bible translations and is the only dictionary that includes the HCSB, NIV, KJV, RSV, NRSV, REB, NASB, ESV, and TEV.

The New Unger's Bible Dictionary, Revised and Expanded, by Merrill F. Unger (Moody, 2006), has been a best seller for almost fifty years. Its 6,700-plus entries reflect the most current scholarship and more than 1,200,000 words are supplemented with detailed essays, colorful photography and maps, and dozens of charts and illustrations to enhance your understanding of God's Word. It is based on the New American Standard Bible.

The Zondervan Encyclopedia of the Bible, edited by Moisés Silva and Merrill C. Tenney (Zondervan, 2008), is excellent and exhaustive. However, its five 1,000-page volumes are a financial investment, so all but very serious students may prefer to use it at a church, public, college, or seminary library.

Unlike a Bible dictionary in the above sense, *Vine's Complete Expository Dictionary of Old and New Testament Words*, by W. E. Vine, Merrill F. Unger, and William White Jr. (Thomas Nelson, 1996), alphabetically lists major words used in the King James Version and defines each Old Testament Hebrew or New Testament Greek word the KJV translates with that English word. *Vine's* lists verse references where that Hebrew or Greek word appears so that you can do your own cross-references and word studies without knowing the original languages.

The Brown-Driver-Briggs Hebrew and English Lexicon, by Francis Brown, C. Briggs, and S. R. Driver (Hendrickson, 1996), is probably the most respected and comprehensive Bible lexicon for Old Testament studies. *BDB* gives not only dictionary definitions for each word but relates each word to its Old Testament usage and categorizes its nuances of meaning.

Bible Atlases and Map Books

A **Bible atlas** can be a great aid to understanding what is going on in a book of the Bible and how geography affected events. Here are a few good choices:

The Hammond Atlas of Bible Lands (Langenscheidt, 2007) packs a ton of resources into just sixty-four pages. Maps, of course, but also photographs, illustrations, and a comprehensive timeline. It includes an introduction to the unique geography of the Holy Land, including terrain, trade routes, vegetation, and climate information.

The New Moody Atlas of the Bible, by Barry J. Beitzel (Moody, 2009), is scholarly, very evangelical, and full of theological text, indexes, and references. Beitzel shows vividly how God prepared the land of Israel perfectly for the acts of salvation He was going to accomplish in it.

Then and Now Bible Maps Insert (Rose, 2008) is a nifty paperback that is sized just right to fit inside your Bible cover. Only forty-four pages long, it features clear plastic overlays of modern-day cities and countries so you can see what nation or city now occupies the Bible setting you are reading about. Every major city of the Bible is included.

For Small-Group Leaders

Discipleship Journal's Best Small-Group Ideas, Volumes 1 and 2 (NavPress, 2005). Each volume is packed with 101 of the best hands-on tips and group-building principles from *Discipleship Journal*'s "Small Group Letter" and "DJ Plus" as well as articles from the magazine. They will help you inject new passion into the life of your small group.

Donahue, Bill. *Leading Life-Changing Small Groups* (Zondervan, 2002). This comprehensive resource is packed with information, practical tips, and insights that will teach you about small-group philosophy and structure, discipleship, conducting meetings, and more.

McBride, Neal F. *How to Build a Small-Groups Ministry* (NavPress, 1994). *How to Build a Small-Groups Ministry* is a time-proven, hands-on workbook for pastors and lay leaders that includes everything you need to know to develop a plan that fits your unique church. Through basic principles, case studies, and worksheets, McBride leads you through twelve logical steps for organizing and administering a small-groups ministry.

McBride, Neal F. *How to Lead Small Groups* (NavPress, 1990). This book covers leadership skills for all kinds of small groups: Bible study, fellowship, task, and support groups. Filled with step-by-step guidance and practical exercises to help you grasp the critical aspects of small-group leadership and dynamics.

Miller, Tara, and Jenn Peppers. *Finding the Flow: A Guide for Leading Small Groups and Gatherings* (IVP Connect, 2008). *Finding the Flow* offers a fresh take on leading small groups by seeking to develop the leader's small-group facilitation skills.

Bible Study Methods

Discipleship Journal's Best Bible Study Methods (NavPress, 2002). This is a collection of thirty-two creative ways to explore Scripture that will help you enjoy studying God's Word more.

Hendricks, Howard, and William Hendricks. *Living by the Book: The Art and Science of Reading the Bible* (Moody, 2007). *Living by the Book* offers a practical three-step process that will help you master simple yet effective inductive methods of observation, interpretation, and application that will make all the difference in your time with God's Word. A workbook by the same title is also available to go along with the book.

The Navigator Bible Studies Handbook (NavPress, 1994). This resource teaches the underlying principles for doing good inductive Bible study, including instructions on doing question-and-answer studies, verse-analysis studies, chapter-analysis studies, and topical studies.

Warren, Rick. *Rick Warren's Bible Study Methods: Twelve Ways You Can Unlock God's Word* (HarperCollins, 2006). Rick Warren offers simple, step-by-step instructions, guiding you through twelve different approaches to studying the Bible for yourself with the goal of becoming more like Jesus.

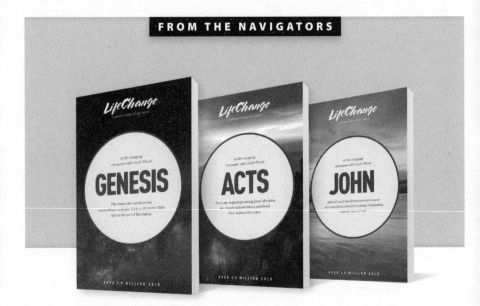